Spelling for Writing

• Contents •

continued

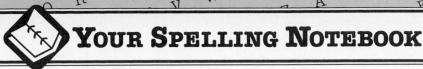

A Personal Word List

Your Spelling Notebook is an easy way to keep track of words that you want to remember. What words should you write in your Spelling Notebook?

- new words from your reading
- words from your writing that you may have trouble spelling
- words that you learn in different school subjects

When should you use your Spelling Notebook?

- when you are trying to think of words to use in your writing
- when you are proofreading, to make sure you have spelled words correctly

..... Keeping a Spelling Notebook ...

The Spelling Notebook has two parts.

In the first part, keep an ABC list of all the words you have trouble spelling or want to remember.

The second part has pages for words that you learn in other subjects. Some words are already listed to help you get started. Write other words that you want to remember from the subject.

Use the extra pages to write words from other subjects, such as music, art, or health.

. . . . Taking your Notebook with you . . .

You may want to pull out pages 77–92 and make them into a booklet to keep with you. Then you will have your Spelling Notebook handy whenever you need to look up words or add new ones.

To make the cover, paste it onto construction paper. Write your name and decorate it any way you want.

Staple the pages together, or punch holes along the sides and tie with yarn.

If you want to keep your Spelling Notebook in a three-ring binder or a folder, paste the cover on the front and put the pages inside.

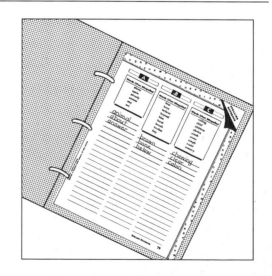

How to Study a Word

1 LOOK at the word.

- What does the word mean?
- What letters are in the word?
- Name and touch each letter.

2 SAY the word.

- Listen for the consonant sounds.
- Listen for the vowel sounds.

3 THINK about the word.

- How is each sound spelled?
- Close your eyes and picture the word.
- What familiar spelling patterns do you see?
- What other words have the same spelling patterns?

4 WRITE the word.

- Think about the sounds and the letters.
- Form the letters correctly.

5 CHECK the spelling.

- Did you spell the word the same way it is spelled in your word list?
- If you did not spell the word correctly, write the word again.

Family Album

Spelling for Writing

It is important to spell correctly when you write to someone else. If you don't, people will have trouble understanding what you mean. Look at this caption a student wrote for a photo in a family scrapbook. Can you tell what it says?

Horay! Tuda my bruthr grajooatd.

Use a dictionary if you are not sure how to spell a word. See how the right spelling helps?

Hurray! Today my brother graduated.

Which words do you often misspell? Starting your own list of these words will help. Then you can easily check each word's spelling when you write.

Starting Your Spelling Notebook

Use the **Spelling Notebook** on pages 77–92 to start your own word list. You might want to keep your Notebook in your writing folder. Then it will be handy when you need it.

SPELLING WORDS

1. fill
2. next
3. jam
4. fell
5. plum
6. plant
7. lunch
8. drop

Your Own Words

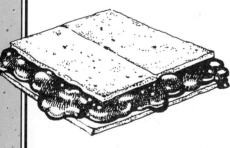 What other words do you need to study for spelling? Add them to My Study List 1 on page 94.

Jam

Name _____

1 Short Vowels

Each Spelling Word has a short vowel sound. A short vowel sound is usually spelled *a, e, i, o,* or *u* and is followed by a consonant sound.

short *a* |ă| **ja**m	short *o* |ŏ| **dro**p
short *e* |ĕ| **ne**xt	short *u* |ŭ| **plu**m
short *i* |ĭ| **fi**ll		

Word Jars **1–8.** Fill Mr. Castle's jars with Spelling Words. Write each Spelling Word on the jar that has the matching vowel sound.

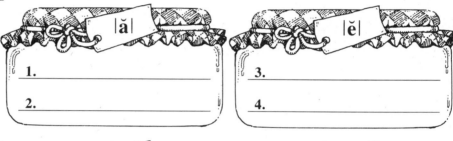

|ă|
1. _____
2. _____

|ĕ|
3. _____
4. _____

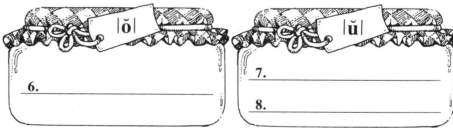

|ĭ|
5. _____

|ŏ|
6. _____

|ŭ|
7. _____
8. _____

Proofreading **9–12.** Find and circle four misspelled Spelling Words in this recipe. Then write each word correctly.

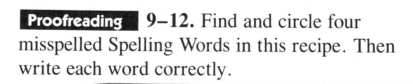

A Cracker Sandwich

First, choose a jam, such as grape or pulm. The nixt step is to get two crackers. Then spread jam between the crackers. Try this treat after luch. It will really fil you up!

9. _____
10. _____
11. _____
12. _____

Developing Meaning

In the Garden Write a Spelling Word to complete each sentence. Each answer has the same short vowel sound as the underlined word.

1. <u>Can</u> you help me ____ a fruit tree?
2. It is <u>not</u> easy to ____ the tree into the hole.
3. <u>Wi</u>ll you please ____ the hole with dirt?
4. Last year I <u>set</u> a tree down, and it ____ over!

1. _____   3. _____

2. _____   4. _____

> ### SPELLING WORDS
>
> 1. fill
> 2. next
> 3. jam
> 4. fell
> 5. plum
> 6. plant
> 7. lunch
> 8. drop
>
> ### Writer's Words from the Story
>
> 9. bread
> 10. crust
> 11. dough
> 12. prepare

Riddles Write a Spelling Word to answer each riddle.
5. I am often served with peanut butter. What am I?
6. I am always after something else. What am I?
7. I am sweet, and I have a pit. What am I?
8. I can't be eaten in the morning or at night. What am I?

5. _____   7. _____

6. _____   8. _____

The Best in Town Write the Writer's Words to complete the paragraph.

Have you tried a loaf of __(9)__ from Pat's Bake Shop? Pat's bakers __(10)__ two hundred loaves each day! Early each morning, the bakers mix flour and water to make soft, thick __(11)__ . The loaves must rise to twice their size before they are put into the oven. Finally, each loaf is baked until it has a crunchy, golden __(12)__ . Try a slice with jam!

9. _____

10. _____

11. _____

12. _____

Spelling and Writing

SPELLING WORDS			
fill	jam	plum	lunch
next	fell	plant	drop

Writer's Words from the Story	
bread	dough
crust	prepare

Plums for Sale Pretend that the Castles want to sell all their plums and the food they made with plums. Write three signs to help the Castles with their sale. Use words from the lists above.

Try a juicy plum today.

Write any words that you had trouble spelling in the ABC section of your Spelling Notebook.

Name _____

2 Vowel-Consonant-e

Each Spelling Word has a long vowel sound spelled with the vowel-consonant-*e* pattern. Notice that the long *u* sound can be said two ways.

long *a* |ā| **game**   long *o* |ō| wh**ole**

long *i* |ī| n**ice**   long *u* |yōō| or |ōō| **huge, tube**

SPELLING WORDS

1. game
2. nice
3. face
4. whole
5. tube
6. side
7. spoke
8. huge

Becky

A Good Sign **1–8.** Each hand below shows a vowel in sign language. Write the Spelling Words that match the vowel-consonant-*e* pattern shown for each hand.

Your Own Words

 What other words do you need to study for spelling? Add them to My Study List 2 on page 94.

|ā| **a** -consonant-**e**

1. _____

2. _____

|ī| **i** -consonant-**e**

3. _____

4. _____

|ō| **o** -consonant-**e**

5. _____

6. _____

|yōō| or |ōō|

u -consonant-**e**

7. _____

8. _____

Proofreading **9–12.** Find and circle four misspelled Spelling Words in this part of a story for a class newspaper. Then write each word correctly.

≡ Class News ≡

Both teams had a nise time at the class kickball game yesterday. The hole class played well, even though nobody scored. Each sid agreed that the day was a huje success!

9. _____

10. _____

11. _____

12. _____

SPELLING WORDS

1. game
2. nice
3. face
4. whole
5. tube
6. side
7. spoke
8. huge

Writer's Words from the Story

9. deaf
10. understand
11. sign
12. practice

Developing Meaning

Word Pairs Write the Spelling Word that completes each pair of sentences.

1. Something tiny is very small.
   Something _____ is very large.
2. You read a book.
   You play a _____.
3. Paint comes in a jar.
   Glue comes in a _____.
4. Your fingers are part of your hand.
   Your eyes are part of your _____.

1. _____ 3. _____

2. _____ 4. _____

Rhyme Time Write the Spelling Word that completes each sentence and rhymes with the underlined word.

5. Maria is baking with lots of <u>spice</u>,
   and now the kitchen smells very _____.
6. Kim stood up and told a <u>joke</u>,
   and we all laughed after she _____!
7. When Mom took me in her car for a <u>ride</u>,
   we went up a big hill and down the other _____.
8. Mr. Egg walked into a <u>pole</u>.
   I glued him together, and now he is _____.

Talking Hands Write the Writer's Words to complete the paragraph.

LOVE

People who cannot hear are __(9)__. They often use their hands to speak in __(10)__ language. Hearing people also use this language so they can __(11)__ and speak to their friends who cannot hear. Anyone can learn this language with a lot of __(12)__.

5. _____

6. _____

7. _____

8. _____

9. _____

10. _____

11. _____

12. _____

Spelling and Writing

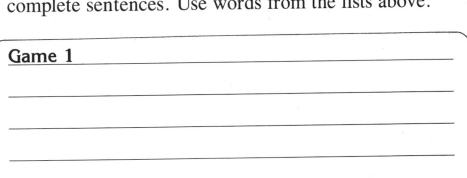

SPELLING WORDS

game	face	tube	spoke
nice	whole	side	huge

Writer's Words from the Story

deaf	sign
understand	practice

Wordless Fun Becky found many ways to play with her hearing friends. Describe three games that you can play with your friends without speaking. Write complete sentences. Use words from the lists above.

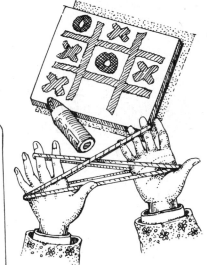

Game 1 _____

_____

_____

_____

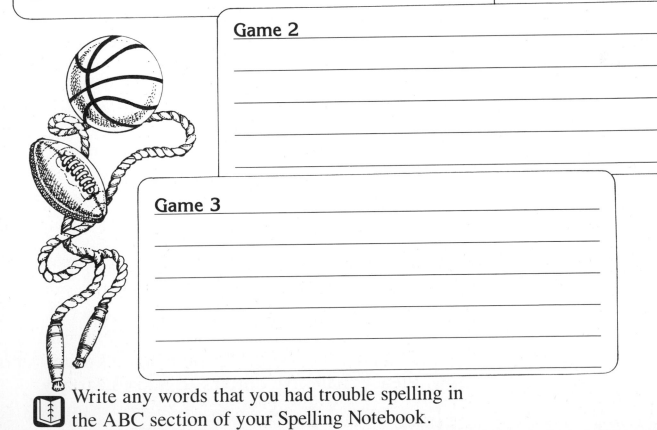

Game 2 _____

_____

_____

_____

Game 3 _____

_____

_____

_____

Write any words that you had trouble spelling in the ABC section of your Spelling Notebook.

SPELLING WORDS

1. need
2. please
3. green
4. lay
5. leave
6. train
7. tray
8. mail

Your Own Words

What other words do you need to study for spelling? Add them to My Study List 3 on page 94.

Name _____

3 Spelling Long a and Long e

Some Spelling Words have the |ā| sound spelled with the pattern *ai* or *ay*.

|ā| tr**ai**n, l**ay**

TIP: Which pattern spells the |ā| sound at the end of a word?

The other Spelling Words have the |ē| sound spelled with the pattern *ea* or *ee*.

|ē| pl**ea**se, n**ee**d

Sew It Up **1–8.** Write the Spelling Words that match the pattern shown on each square in Tanya's quilt.

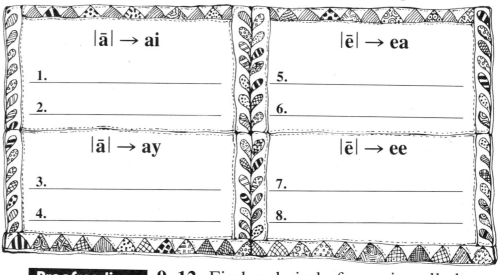

|ā| → ai

1. _____
2. _____

|ē| → ea

5. _____
6. _____

|ā| → ay

3. _____
4. _____

|ē| → ee

7. _____
8. _____

Proofreading **9–12.** Find and circle four misspelled Spelling Words in this announcement. Then write each word correctly.

Come with the Fun Club to the Craft Museum next Saturday. Two things you will see are a carved, wooden trey and a grean quilt that is ninety years old! You nede to sign up now. Please male five dollars to Mary Li today.

9. _____
10. _____
11. _____
12. _____

Name _____

Developing Meaning

Hink Pinks   Write the Spelling Word that answers the question and rhymes with the given word.

Example: What does an unplanted garden have?

a seed _____   *need*

1. What do you call a railroad car that delivers oats?
   a grain ____
2. What is a long, skinny vegetable that is the color of a leaf? a ____ bean
3. What do you call a bucket filled with post cards?
   a ____ pail
4. What do you call a horse's serving dish?
   a hay ____

1. _____   3. _____

2. _____   4. _____

Crazy Quilt   Write the Spelling Word that completes each sentence.

5. Hundreds of cloth squares ____ all over the rug.
6. "I ____ more thread for this quilt," said Ruth.
7. Ruth couldn't ____ the baby alone in the room.
8. She called to her sister, "Will you bring me more white thread, ____?"

5. _____   7. _____

6. _____   8. _____

A Handmade Treasure   Write the Writer's Words to complete the paragraph.

   Do you want a bed covering that you will always prize? Make a __(9)__! First, get many pieces of colorful cloth, such as cotton or another __(10)__. Cut a four-sided __(11)__ from each piece. Put all the pieces together and __(12)__ them with a needle and thread. Stuff the cover with feathers. You will be so cozy!

SPELLING WORDS

1. need
2. please
3. green
4. lay
5. leave
6. train
7. tray
8. mail

Writer's Words from the Story

9. quilt
10. sew
11. square
12. material

9. _____
10. _____
11. _____
12. _____

Spelling and Writing

SPELLING WORDS			
need	green	leave	tray
please	lay	train	mail

Writer's Words from the Story	
quilt	square
sew	material

Make It Yourself Tanya helped her mother and grandmother make a quilt. Think of something that you made by hand, and tell how to make it. Give step-by-step directions. Use words from the lists above.

Step 1: _____

_____

_____

Step 2: _____

_____

_____

Step 3: _____

_____

_____

Step 4: _____

_____

_____

Write any words that you had trouble spelling in the ABC section of your Spelling Notebook.

Name _____

Spelling Review

Write Spelling Words from the list on this page to answer each question.

A short vowel sound is usually spelled *a, e, i, o,* or *u* and is followed by a consonant sound.

1–5. Which five words have a short vowel sound?

1. _____ 4. _____

2. _____ 5. _____

3. _____

A long vowel sound is often spelled with the vowel-consonant-*e* pattern.

6–8. Which three words have a long vowel sound spelled with the vowel-consonant-*e* pattern? Underline the pattern that spells the long vowel sound in each word.

6. _____ 8. _____

7. _____

|ā| m**ai**l, tr**ay** |ē| l**ea**ve, gr**ee**n

9–10. Which two words have the |ā| sound? Underline the pattern that spells the |ā| sound in each word.

9. _____ 10. _____

11–12. Which two words have the |ē| sound? Underline the pattern that spells the |ē| sound in each word.

11. _____

12. _____

SPELLING WORDS

next
spoke
lay
plum
side
fill
need
train
drop
huge
jam
please

Name _____

Spelling Spree

Write Spelling Words from the list on this page to complete the activities.

Puzzle Play Write a word for each clue.

13. where your nose is
14. kickball or softball
15. stamped envelopes
16. the opposite of *nasty*
17. the noontime meal
18. what you carry food on
19. what toothpaste comes in
20. the color of grass
21. to put in the ground
22. to go away from
23. not half, but ___
24. rhymes with *tell*

What activity does this memory album show? Find out by writing the letters in the boxes in order.

_ _ _ _ _ _ _ _   _ _ _ _ _ _

25. _____
26. _____
27. _____
28. _____
29. _____
30. _____

In the News Write the word that completes each headline. Begin each word with a capital letter.

25. Paint Truck Spill Turns Main Street ___
26. South Haven Wins Soccer ___
27. Students Will ___ Next Week for Class Trip
28. Children Find Rock That ___ from Space!
29. Post Office Discovers Lost ___ from 1895!
30. Contest Winner Paints Clown's New ___

IT'S MAGIC

Reading and Spelling

As you read the stories in this theme, you will find many new and magical words!

fantastic   vanish   **presto**

hypnotized   **marvel**   miracle

Look for new words whenever you read. Once you learn these words, they will start popping up everywhere you look. Use them to add magic to your own writing!

The Great Gordo put on a **fantastic** magic show for our school. He made a teacher **vanish**. Then **presto** — the teacher appeared again!

Keeping Your Spelling Notebook

You may not always remember how to spell new words. Add them to your own word list in your **Spelling Notebook**.

From time to time, look at the words you have written in your Spelling Notebook. Choose some to add to the "My Own Words" part of the Study Lists.

SPELLING WORDS

1. tie
2. tight
3. coat
4. night
5. own
6. snow
7. die
8. float

Your Own Words

What other words do you need to study for spelling? Add them to My Study List 5 on page 96.

Name _____

5 Spelling Long i and Long o

Some Spelling Words have the |ī| sound spelled with the pattern *igh* or *ie*.

|ī| **tigh**t, **tie**

The other Spelling Words have the |ō| sound spelled with the pattern *oa* or *ow*.

|ō| c**oa**t, **ow**n

Lock and Key   **1–8.** Write the Spelling Words that match the pattern shown on each of Houdini's locks.

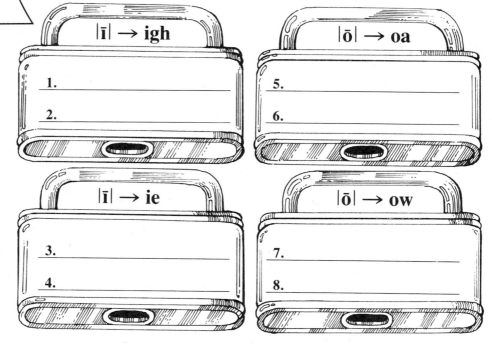

|ī| → igh

1. _____
2. _____

|ō| → oa

5. _____
6. _____

|ī| → ie

3. _____
4. _____

|ō| → ow

7. _____
8. _____

Proofreading   **9–12.** Find and circle four misspelled Spelling Words in this poem. Then write each word correctly.

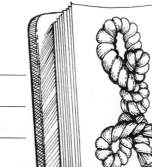

Can You Do This?

Can you take off your own cote
If I tye your hands up tihgt?
I saw a man do a trick like that
In a magic show last nite!

9. _____
10. _____
11. _____
12. _____

Developing Meaning

Crossword Chain 1–8. Help Houdini escape! Break this puzzle chain by writing the Spelling Word that fits each clue.

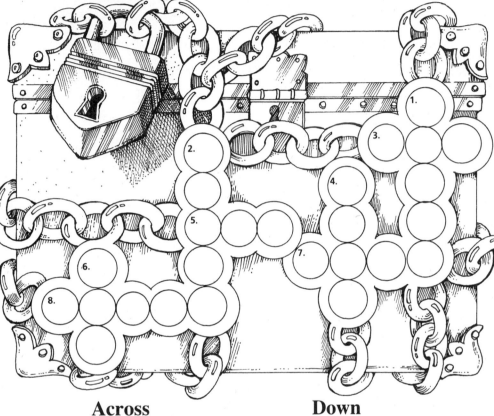

SPELLING WORDS

1. tie
2. tight
3. coat
4. night
5. own
6. snow
7. die
8. float

Writer's Words from the Story

9. magic
10. stunt
11. escape
12. vanish

Across

3. to make a knot
5. to have
7. what you might wear on a cold day
8. snug

Down

1. a time to sleep
2. what a boat does
4. frozen flakes
6. what some flowers do in cold weather

Hatti Huzzini Write the Writer's Words to complete the paragraph.

Last night we went to a show and saw tricks that seemed like __(9)__ ! Hattie Huzzini got into a box, and the box was tied up with chains. Then the box was opened. No one was there! How did Hattie disappear, or __(10)__ , into the air? Not everyone can __(11)__ from chains. I do not know how she did a __(12)__ like that!

9. _____

10. _____

11. _____

12. _____

Spelling and Writing

SPELLING WORDS

tie	coat	own	die
tight	night	snow	float

Writer's Words from the Story

magic	escape
stunt	vanish

Do Not Miss This Show! Pretend that you live in a big city. The year is 1924, and the Great Houdini is coming to town! Where will he perform? What tricks will he do? Write a newspaper ad for the show. Use words from the lists above.

The Daily Sun
October 23, 1924

Write any words that you had trouble spelling in the ABC section of your Spelling Notebook.

Name _____

6 Vowel Sounds in count and boy

Some Spelling Words have the vowel sound that you hear in *count*. This sound is written as |ou|. It is often spelled with the pattern *ow* or *ou*.

|ou| cr**ow**d, c**ou**nt

The other Spelling Words have the vowel sound that you hear in *boy*. This sound is written as |oi|. It is spelled with the pattern *oi* or *oy*.

|oi| c**oi**n, b**oy**

TIP: How is |oi| spelled at the end of a word?

Harry's Hoops   **1–8.** Write each Spelling Word next to the correct sound and spelling pattern.

1. _____

2. _____

5. _____

6. _____

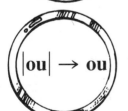
3. _____

4. _____

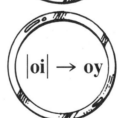
7. _____

8. _____

Proofreading   **9–12.** Find and circle four misspelled Spelling Words in this post card from India. Then write each word correctly.

Dear Ken,

Today I heard noize from a croud outside my window. I looked out and saw a magician with a toi snake. Suddenly the snake made a hissing sownd at a boy! The snake was real!

9. _____

10. _____

11. _____

12. _____

Theme 2 It's Magic THE FLOATING PRINCESS   **23**

SPELLING WORDS

1. count
2. bow
3. boy
4. coin
5. toy
6. sound
7. crowd
8. noise

Your Own Words

What other words do you need to study for spelling? Add them to My Study List 6 on page 96.

The Floating Princess

Developing Meaning

SPELLING WORDS

1. count
2. bow
3. boy
4. coin
5. toy
6. sound
7. crowd
8. noise

Writer's Words from the Story

9. clever
10. perform
11. curtain
12. marvel

Word Pairs   Write the Spelling Word that completes each pair of sentences.

1. You add numbers.
   You ___ money.
2. A hammer is a tool.
   A yo-yo is a ___.
3. Put a dollar in your wallet.
   Put a ___ in your piggy bank.
4. Three people are a group.
   Fifty people are a ___.

1. _____   3. _____

2. _____   4. _____

Give a Command!   Write the Spelling Word that completes each command a magician might make.

5. I need help. Come up here, little ___!
6. Stop all that loud ___, please!
7. Pull this rope at the ___ of music.
8. When the audience claps, take a ___.

Keep Them Guessing!   Write the Writer's Words to complete the paragraph.

The crowd has come to see the famous Indian rope trick. The show begins when the __(9)__ rises. People __(10)__ at the magician's skill. He is not only skillful, he's very __(11)__. He waits until the end of the show to __(12)__ the rope trick. It works! The crowd cheers!

5. _____

6. _____

7. _____

8. _____

9. _____

10. _____

11. _____

12. _____

Spelling and Writing

SPELLING WORDS

count	boy	toy	crowd
bow	coin	sound	noise

Writer's Words from the Story

clever   curtain
perform   marvel

You Are the Author! Pretend that you are writing a book about magic. Write three different titles that will make people want to read your book. Begin the first, last, and each important word with a capital letter. Use words from the lists above.

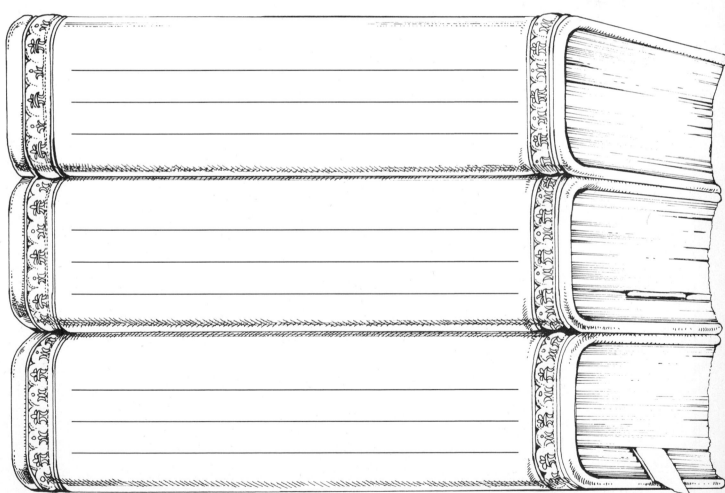

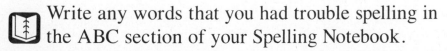 Write any words that you had trouble spelling in the ABC section of your Spelling Notebook.

SPELLING WORDS

1. walk
2. straw
3. raw
4. caught
5. ball
6. bought
7. taught
8. thought

Your Own Words

What other words do you need to study for spelling? Add them to My Study List 7 on page 96.

Name _____

7 The Vowel Sound in ball

Each Spelling Word has the vowel sound that you hear in *ball*. This sound is written as |ô|. It can be spelled with the pattern *aw*, *a* before *l*, *ough*, or *augh*.

|ô| str**aw**, w**a**lk, b**ough**t, c**augh**t

Top Hats   **1–8.** Write each Spelling Word on the hat that has the matching pattern for the |ô| sound.

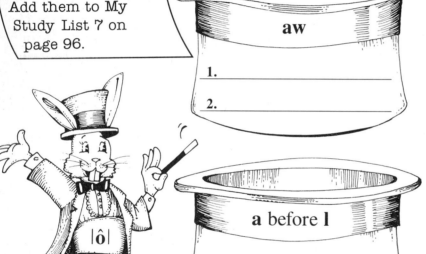

aw

1. _____
2. _____

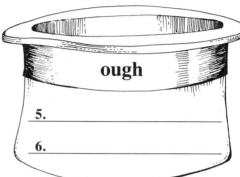

ough

5. _____
6. _____

a before **l**

3. _____
4. _____

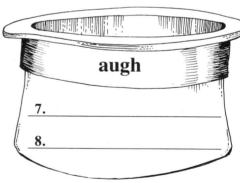

augh

7. _____
8. _____

Proofreading   **9–12.** Find and circle four misspelled Spelling Words in this story about a young magician. Then write each word correctly.

9. _____

10. _____

11. _____

12. _____

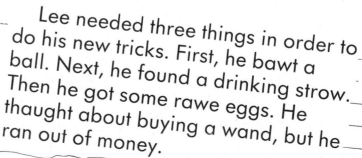

Lee needed three things in order to do his new tricks. First, he bawt a ball. Next, he found a drinking strow. Then he got some rawe eggs. He thaught about buying a wand, but he ran out of money.

Developing Meaning

New Tricks   Write Spelling Words to complete these
sentences about a young magician named Kara.

1. Kara had to ____ two miles to the bookstore.
2. She ____ herself a book about magic.
3. After reading the book, Kara ____ about learning
   a new magic trick.
4. She felt proud after she ____ herself the trick.

1. _____   3. _____

2. _____   4. _____

The Magic Hen   Write Spelling Words to complete
this funny rhyme about a magic hen.

My hen was in her nest of __(5)__ .
She laid an egg. The egg was __(6)__ .
She tossed the egg just like a __(7)__ !
I __(8)__ the egg. It did not fall.
The egg turned blue, and then—surprise!
It disappeared before my eyes!

5. _____   7. _____

6. _____   8. _____

**SPELLING
WORDS**

1. walk
2. straw
3. raw
4. caught
5. ball
6. bought
7. taught
8. thought

**Writer's Words
from the Story**

9. secret
10. expect
11. disappear
12. impossible

Clever Old Dog   Write the Writer's Words to
complete the paragraph.

"Do not count on, or __(9)__ , an old dog to learn new
tricks," said Dad. "That is very hard, if not __(10)__ !"

"My dog Tex is awfully clever," replied Pedro.

Pedro had a __(11)__ that his father didn't know. He
had taught Tex to catch a ball! He called Tex. Tex did
not come.

"I see!" Dad laughed. "You taught Tex to __(12)__ !"

9. _____

10. _____

11. _____

12. _____

Spelling and Writing

walk	raw	ball	taught
straw	caught	bought	thought

Writer's Words from the Story

secret	disappear
expect	impossible

Fancy Finish Pretend that you and your friend Max are on the phone. You are deciding what trick to do at the end of your magic show. Write down your conversation. Use words from the lists above.

You: _____

_____

_____

Max: _____

_____

_____

You: _____

_____

_____

Max: _____

_____

_____

 Write any words that you had trouble spelling in the ABC section of your Spelling Notebook.

Name _____

Spelling Review

Write Spelling Words from the list on this page to answer each question.

Remember │ī│ n**igh**t, d**ie**   │ō│ fl**oa**t, **ow**n

1–2. Which two words have the │ī│ sound? Underline the pattern that spells the │ī│ sound in each word.

1. _____   2. _____

3–4. Which two words have the │ō│ sound? Underline the pattern that spells the │ō│ sound in each word.

3. _____   4. _____

Remember │ou│ b**ow**, s**ou**nd   │oi│ n**oi**se, t**oy**

5–6. Which two words have the │ou│ sound? Underline the pattern that spells the │ou│ sound in each word.

5. _____   6. _____

7–8. Which two words have the │oi│ sound? Underline the pattern that spells the │oi│ sound in each word.

7. _____   8. _____

Remember │ô│ r**aw**, b**a**ll, b**ough**t, c**augh**t

9–12. Which four words have the │ô│ sound? Underline the pattern that spells the │ô│ sound in each word.

SPELLING
WORDS

taught
snow
coin
tight
crowd
straw
tie
boy
count
thought
walk
coat

9. _____

10. _____

11. _____

12. _____

Name _____

own
die
caught
night
toy
ball
sound
bought
raw
noise
float
bow

Spelling Spree

Write Spelling Words from the list on this page to complete the activities.

Magic Scarves   **13–18.** Find and circle six words on the magic scarves. Then write each word correctly.

13. _____   16. _____

14. _____   17. _____

15. _____   18. _____

Escape Hatch   Climb down the pole to the hidden door in the floor by writing a word for each clue.

Clues

19. rhymes with *round*
20. opposite of *live*
21. not threw, but ____
22. not cooked
23. has the |oi| sound spelled *oi*
24. what a doll is

19. __ __ __ __ __

20. __ __ __

21. __ __ __ __ __ __

22. __ __ __ __

23. __ __ __ __ __

24. __ __ __

Just for Fun   Read down the pole to find a word that tells about this door! Circle the word.

A VISIT TO THE SOUTHWEST

Writing and Spelling

Always use the clearest words possible when you write. What if you are not sure how to spell a word? Use it anyway! Spell it as well as you can. You can fix any spelling mistakes when you proofread.

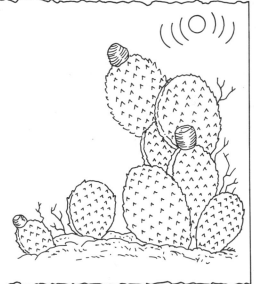

Last summer my family visited New
delicious
Mexico. I ate a (delishus) kind of bread
tortilla   *prickly*
called a (torteeyah.) I saw lots of (prikly)
fascinating
cactuses. It was a (fasinating) trip!

After you are done writing, circle the words you may have misspelled. Check their spellings in a dictionary. Then write the words correctly.

Keeping Your Spelling Notebook

Look at your own writing. Add any words that you misspell to your own word list in your **Spelling Notebook**.

Look over the words in your list from time to time, and choose five words. Use the How to Study a Word steps on page 5 to help you learn to spell the words.

1. summer
2. Sunday
3. invite
4. dinner
5. happen
6. number
7. basket
8. rabbit

Your Own Words

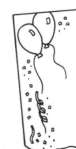 What other words do you need to study for spelling? Add them to My Study List 9 on page 98.

1. _____
2. _____
3. _____
4. _____
5. _____
6. _____
7. _____
8. _____

Name _____

9 The VCCV Pattern

Each Spelling Word has the vowel-consonant-consonant-vowel (VCCV) pattern. Divide a word with this pattern between the two consonants to find the syllables. Look for spelling patterns you have learned. Spell the word by syllables.

```
V C | C V          V C | C V
s u m | m e r      S u n | d a y
```

Syllable Painting   Be an artist! Finish the painting by writing the missing syllable for each Spelling Word. Then write the complete word.

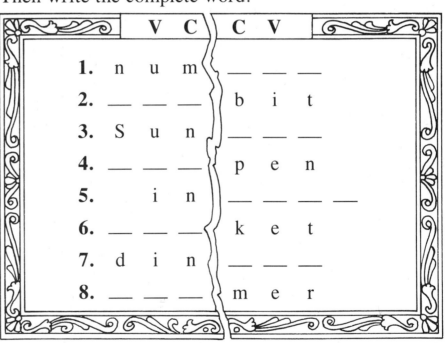

V	C		C	V
1. n	u	m	___ ___ ___
2. ___ ___ ___		b	i	t
3. S	u	n	___ ___ ___
4. ___ ___ ___		p	e	n
5. ___	i	n	___ ___ ___
6. ___ ___ ___		k	e	t
7. d	i	n	___ ___ ___
8. ___ ___ ___		m	e	r

Proofreading   9–12. Find and circle four misspelled Spelling Words in this part of an invitation. Then write each word correctly.

Dear Simon,
We invit you to a party at our sumer cabin. Rosa Diaz is having birthday number nine! Please come for dinner on Sonday, July 11.

9. _____
10. _____
11. _____
12. _____

Developing Meaning

Party Time! Write a Spelling Word to take the place
of each underlined word.

1. How many people did Erin <u>ask</u> to her party?
2. The party was in the back yard because it was a
   warm <u>June</u> day.
3. The birthday candles were shaped like a <u>nine</u>.
4. We each had a little straw <u>container</u> to hold the
   prizes that fell from the piñata.
5. How did Louis <u>come</u> to find the most prizes?
6. Erin's favorite birthday gift was a little white
   <u>bunny</u> that hopped around the yard.

1. _____   4. _____

2. _____   5. _____

3. _____   6. _____

**SPELLING
WORDS**

1. summer
2. Sunday
3. invite
4. dinner
5. happen
6. number
7. basket
8. rabbit

**Writer's Words
from the Story**

9. artist
10. drawing
11. scene
12. favorite

Classifying Write the Spelling Word that belongs in
each group.

7. breakfast, lunch, ___
8. bag, box, ___
9. Friday, Saturday, ___
10. winter, spring, ___

7. _____

8. _____

9. _____

10. _____

Animal Pictures Write the Writer's Words to
complete the paragraph.

When Carl was young, he always carried a pencil
and paper so that he could practice __(11)__ anywhere.
One day he saw two dogs playing in a field. He
sketched the __(12)__ he was watching. Carl decided that
making animal pictures was his __(13)__ way to spend
time. He became an __(14)__ when he grew up so that he
could always do what he loved best.

11. _____

12. _____

13. _____

14. _____

Spelling and Writing

SPELLING WORDS

summer	invite	happen	basket
Sunday	dinner	number	rabbit

Writer's Words from the Story

artist	scene
drawing	favorite

What's Happening? The author of *Family Pictures* enjoyed telling about the pictures she painted. Look at the pictures below. Write sentences to tell about each one. Use words from the lists above.

1. _____

_____

_____

2. _____

_____

_____

 Write any words that you had trouble spelling in the ABC section of your Spelling Notebook.

Name _____

10 Compound Words

Each Spelling Word is a **compound word.** A compound word is made up of two or more shorter words.

grand + **father** = grandfather   **may** + **be** = maybe

Word Farolito Make a compound word farolito. Draw lines between the candle and the bag to form Spelling Words. Then write the words you made.

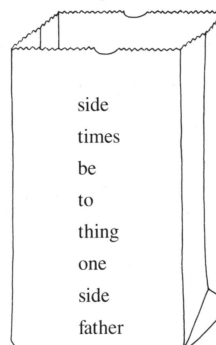

1. some	side
2. grand	times
3. any	be
4. some	to
5. in	thing
6. may	one
7. in	side
8. out	father

SPELLING WORDS

1. grandfather
2. maybe
3. inside
4. outside
5. into
6. something
7. anyone
8. sometimes

Your Own Words

What other words do you need to study for spelling? Add them to My Study List 10 on page 98.

1. _____
2. _____
3. _____
4. _____
5. _____
6. _____
7. _____
8. _____

Proofreading **9–12.** Find and circle four misspelled Spelling Words in this diary entry. Then write each word correctly.

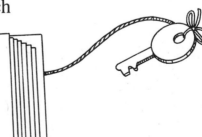

January 3   Today I walked on the beach with my granfather. I do not like to go outdoors at all during the winter, but Gramps says you cannot stay insid and watch the sea. Sometimes it is so cold that we do not see anyone else on the beach. I think mabe Gramps likes those days the best.

9. _____
10. _____
11. _____
12. _____

Developing Meaning

SPELLING WORDS

1. grandfather
2. maybe
3. inside
4. outside
5. into
6. something
7. anyone
8. sometimes

Writer's Words from the Story

9. gift
10. visit
11. decorate
12. celebrate

Clock Clues   Write a Spelling Word to complete each sentence. Match the time in the sentence with the two words in the clock that show that time.

Example: Will ____ be home at 9:35?   *anyone*

1. We go ____ for recess at 10:15.
2. I ____ get out of school at 2:00.
3. I will help my ____ milk the cows at 4:30.
4. Mom calls us ____ for dinner at 5:15.
5. I think ____ I will go to the 8:05 movie.

Holiday Questions   Write a Spelling Word to complete each question.

6. Happy Halloween! Did you carve a pumpkin and put a candle ____ it?
7. April Fool! Did you do ____ silly today?
8. Does ____ here want to be my Valentine?
9. It is July Fourth! Did you see fireworks shoot ____ the air?
10. Did your grandmother and your ____ come to your house for Thanksgiving dinner?

A Special Day   Write the Writer's Words to complete the paragraph.

All week Chen had helped to __(11)__ the house with balloons and pictures. Today Chen's grandmother and grandfather would arrive for a lengthy __(12)__. The whole family would be there to __(13)__ the long marriage of Chen's grandparents. Chen wrote a poem about their forty years together. This was his __(14)__ to them.

1. _____
2. _____
3. _____
4. _____
5. _____
6. _____
7. _____
8. _____
9. _____
10. _____
11. _____
12. _____
13. _____
14. _____

Spelling and Writing

SPELLING WORDS			
grandfather	inside	into	anyone
maybe	outside	something	sometimes

Writer's Words from the Story
gift   decorate
visit   celebrate

Holiday Greetings Luz made one hundred farolitos to decorate the Christmas night. Write sentences that tell how you might decorate a classroom bulletin board for one of your favorite holidays. Use words from the lists above. Be sure to name the holiday!

☆ HAPPY HOLIDAYS ☆

_____

_____

_____

_____

_____

_____

_____

_____

_____

 Write any words that you had trouble spelling in the ABC section of your Spelling Notebook.

SPELLING WORDS

1. taking
2. dropped
3. planned
4. diving
5. closed
6. begged
7. saved
8. chopping

Your Own Words

What other words do you need to study for spelling? Add them to My Study List 11 on page 98.

Name _____

11 Words Ending with -ed or -ing

Each Spelling Word is made up of a base word and the ending *-ed* or *-ing*. A **base word** is a word to which an ending may be added. When a base word ends with *e*, drop the *e* before adding *-ed* or *-ing*.

take − e + ing = tak**ing**

When a base word ends with one vowel and one consonant, the consonant is usually doubled before *-ed* or *-ing* is added.

drop + p + ed = dro**pped**

Eagle Endings **1–8.** Join the base words and endings on the eagle to make Spelling Words. Then write each word under the correct heading.

save + ed
dive + ing
drop + ed
take + ing
beg + ed
chop + ing
plan + ed
close + ed

Drop the final *e*.

1. _____
2. _____
3. _____
4. _____

Double the final consonant.

5. _____
6. _____
7. _____
8. _____

Proofreading **9–12.** Find and circle four misspelled Spelling Words in this camping log. Then write each word correctly.

Saturday, June 5

Today I went on a nature walk. I saw a ranger chapping logs, a huge rock that droped from a cliff, and a divving hawk. When I got back to my tent, there was a bear takeing my food! I saved myself by hiding until he left!

9. _____
10. _____
11. _____
12. _____

Developing Meaning

SPELLING WORDS

1. taking
2. dropped
3. planned
4. diving
5. closed
6. begged
7. saved
8. chopping

Writer's Words from the Story

9. legend
10. ancient
11. remember
12. forever

Synonym Sentences   Write the Spelling Word that has almost the same meaning as each underlined word.

1. Emma was <u>cutting</u> down a dead cactus.
2. The door of the cabin was <u>shut</u>.
3. A ripe orange <u>fell</u> from the tree.
4. Todd is <u>carrying</u> a backpack on the hike.

1. _____   3. _____

2. _____   4. _____

Animal Play   Write Spelling Words to complete the sentences in this skit.

Moose: Did I just see you and Hawk __(5)__ down through the sky like an airplane?

Frog: Yes. I asked him for a ride, and at first he refused. He finally gave in after I __(6)__ him for ten minutes!

Moose: I guess he had not __(7)__ a trip like that.

Frog: No, but it __(8)__ me from taking a long hop!

5. _____

6. _____

7. _____

8. _____

How a Flower Got Its Name   Write the Writer's Words to complete the paragraph.

Long ago, in __(9)__ times, Indian storytellers told a tale that will last __(10)__. In this __(11)__, a young artist found paint-filled brushes on a hill one day. He used the brushes to paint a picture of the sunset. When he finished, the boy left the brushes behind. The next day the hillside was covered with beautiful wildflowers the color of a sunset. Now when these orange flowers bloom each spring we __(12)__ the boy. In fact, we call this flower the Indian paintbrush.

9. _____

10. _____

11. _____

12. _____

Spelling and Writing

SPELLING WORDS			
taking	planned	closed	saved
dropped	diving	begged	chopping

Writer's Words from the Story	
legend	remember
ancient	forever

What's the Story? Indian legends often explain why animals are the way they are. The books on this page show the titles of some animal legends. Choose one book and circle it. Pretend that you are that animal and draw a picture of yourself. Then tell your story in the speech balloon. Use words from the lists above.

Draw your picture below.

Write any words that you had trouble spelling in the ABC section of your Spelling Notebook.

Name _____

Spelling Review

Write Spelling Words from the list on this page to answer each question.

grandfather
happen
taking
begged
basket
anyone
saved
sometimes
planned
rabbit

Remember

V C | C V   V C | C V
n u m | b e r   i n | v i t e

1–3. Which three words are spelled with the VCCV pattern and have two syllables?

1. _____   3. _____

2. _____

Remember

A compound word is made up of two or more shorter words.

4–6. Which three words are compound words?

4. _____   6. _____

5. _____

Remember

drop + p + ed = dro**pped**
dive − e + ing = div**ing**

7–8. In which two words do you double the final consonant of the base word before adding -*ed* or -*ing*?

7. _____   8. _____

9–10. In which two words do you drop the final *e* from the base word before adding -*ed* or -*ing*?

9. _____   10. _____

Theme 3 A Visit to the Southwest REVIEW   **41**

Name _____

into
summer
Sunday
chopping
closed
number
maybe
inside
something
dinner
dropped
invite
diving
outside

Spelling Spree

Write Spelling Words from the list on this page to complete the activities.

Word Wall Write a word inside the stones to answer each riddle.

11. I am one part of a swimming contest. What am I?
12. I can be eaten, but I'm not a snack. What am I?
13. I am never opened. What am I?
14. I am the opposite of *nothing*. What am I?
15. I am the warmest time of year. What am I?
16. I am the opposite of *out of*. What am I?
17. I am the same as *perhaps*. What am I?
18. I am never outdoors. What am I?
19. I can help you count. What am I?

Secret Message: Read the letters in the gray stones to answer this riddle.

In the Southwest, what can you enjoy that you cannot see?

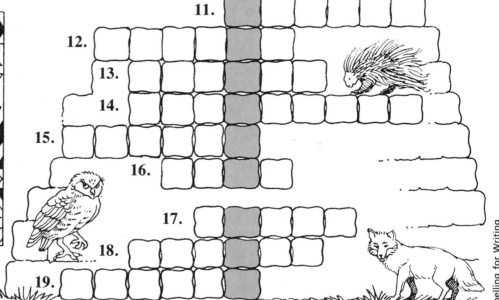

Tongue Twisters Write a word to complete each tongue twister. Then quickly say each sentence to a partner.

20. Otto and Orville own the old oak that is ___.
21. Did Inez ___ Irwin to ice skate in an igloo?
22. Charles was ___ chunks of cheese and chicken.
23. Sue sang a silly song on a sunny September ___.
24. Drew ___ his drink when a dragon drove by.

20. _____
21. _____
22. _____
23. _____
24. _____

BEWARE! TROUBLE AHEAD

Reading and Spelling

Reading is a great way to discover words. Make word discoveries as you read the stories in this theme.

When Miss Hester came to the door Alan **blurted** out his **incredible** story.
(from *The Garden of Abdul Gasazi*)

"How would you like to be the first one to receive this **unique** treatment?"
(from *Doctor De Soto*)

After you discover a word, use it often to make it yours!

This book is about an **incredible** castle that floats in the sky!

The pictures are really **unique**! They're so different!

Keeping Your Spelling Notebook

As you discover new words in your reading, write them in your own word list in your **Spelling Notebook**.

Look over the words in your Notebook. Which words have familiar spelling patterns? Choose ten words, and use those spelling patterns to help you learn your words.

43

1. happy
2. only
3. very
4. ready
5. any
6. heavy
7. baby
8. funny

Your Own Words

What other words do you need to study for spelling? Add them to My Study List 13 on page 100.

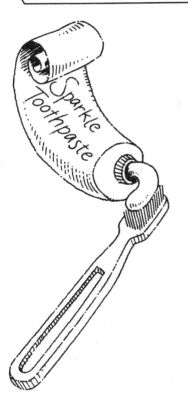

Name _____

13 The Final Sound in happy

Each Spelling Word has two syllables. The second syllable in each word has the final |ē| sound. In two-syllable words, the final |ē| sound may be spelled *y*.

final |ē| happ**y**, onl**y**

Tooth Pick Complete each Spelling Word by writing the letter that spells the final |ē| sound. Then write the words you made.

1. heav
2. an
3. bab
4. ver

5. funn
6. read
7. onl
8. happ

1. _____
2. _____
3. _____
4. _____

5. _____
6. _____
7. _____
8. _____

Proofreading 9–12. Find and circle four misspelled Spelling Words in this ad. Write each word correctly.

I will be very hapy to care for your teeth. I am reddy to see you Monday through Friday. I can take care of eny grownup or babey.
Call Doctor Tiger, Dentist
555-FANG

9. _____
10. _____
11. _____
12. _____

Developing Meaning

Open Wider!   You are in a dentist's chair. The dentist talks, but you cannot reply. Write a Spelling Word to complete each question the dentist asks.

1. Didn't you have your teeth checked ___ last month?
2. Are you almost ___ for me to begin?
3. Has that tooth given you ___ trouble at all?
4. Do you brush your teeth ___ often?

1. _____   3. _____

2. _____   4. _____

Loose Tooth   Write the Spelling Word that means the opposite of each underlined word and makes sense in the sentence.

5. I have gone to my dentist since I was a <u>grownup</u>.
6. The dentist is always <u>sad</u> to see me.
7. She tells me a <u>serious</u> joke to make me laugh.
8. Then the dentist puts me in her big, <u>light</u> chair.

Beware of the Lion   Write the Writer's Words to complete the paragraph.

Doctor Lion was hard at work in his __(9)__ . He made a set of sharp false teeth and decided to __(10)__ them with a brush. He put the teeth in his lower __(11)__ and gave a scary smile. Just then a tiny bunny came in.

"Oops!" said the bunny. "You are not the __(12)__ who fixes *my* teeth!"

SPELLING WORDS

1. happy
2. only
3. very
4. ready
5. any
6. heavy
7. baby
8. funny

Writer's Words from the Story

9. dentist
10. office
11. jaw
12. polish

5. _____

6. _____

7. _____

8. _____

9. _____

10. _____

11. _____

12. _____

Spelling and Writing

SPELLING WORDS

| happy | very | any | baby |
| only | ready | heavy | funny |

Writer's Words from the Story

| dentist | jaw |
| office | polish |

Dental Work   Your dentist needs help! He wants you to answer his telephone and make appointments for his patients. Write sentences that tell what he will be doing each hour. Use words from the lists above.

12:00 _____

_____

1:00 _____

_____

2:00 _____

_____

3:00 _____

_____

4:00 _____

_____

5:00 _____

_____

Write any words that you had trouble spelling in the ABC section of your Spelling Notebook.

Name _____

14 Words That End with er or le

Each Spelling Word has a weak vowel sound called the **schwa** sound. This sound is written as |ə|.

Some Spelling Words have the |ə| + r sounds that you hear in *water*. These sounds are often spelled with the pattern *er*.

|ər| wat**er**

The other Spelling Words have the |ə| + l sounds that you hear in *little*. These sounds can be spelled with the pattern *le*.

|əl| litt**le**

Your Own Words

What other words do you need to study for spelling? Add them to My Study List 14 on page 100.

Plenty for Po Po 1–8. Help Shang, Tao, and Paotze gather gingko nuts for Po Po. Write each Spelling Word on the basket that has the matching sounds.

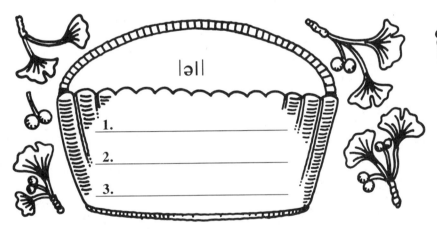

|əl|

1. _____
2. _____
3. _____

|ər|

4. _____
5. _____
6. _____
7. _____
8. _____

Proofreading 9–12. Find and circle four misspelled Spelling Words in this news story. Then write each word correctly.

Boy Is Hero in House Fire

A candel tipped over by accident last night. A fire started undr a table. A little boy saved his granmother and himself. He used watter to put out the fire.

9. _____
10. _____
11. _____
12. _____

Theme 4 Beware! Trouble Ahead LON PO PO   **47**

Lon Po Po

Name _____

SPELLING WORDS

1. water
2. other
3. little
4. under
5. enter
6. candle
7. grandmother
8. tumble

Writer's Words from the Story

9. wolf
10. growl
11. pretend
12. strength

Developing Meaning

Going to Grandpa's You and a friend are playing a game. To win you must get to Grandpa's Door without drawing the Wolf Card. Write Spelling Words to complete these game cards.

1. Find a tiny, ____ frog. Move ahead one space.	3. Jump over Wolf. You have no ____ way out!
2. Trip and ____ down a hill. Lose your turn.	4. You may ____ Grandpa's Door. You win!

1. _____   3. _____

2. _____   4. _____

Word Pairs Write a Spelling Word to complete each pair of sentences.

5. Your mother's father is your grandfather.
   Your mother's mother is your ____.
6. You eat bread.
   You drink ____.
7. You turn on a lamp.
   You light a ____.
8. The opposite of *hot* is *cold*.
   The opposite of *over* is ____.

5. _____

6. _____

7. _____

8. _____

Danger at the Door! Write the Writer's Words to complete the paragraph.

One day a hungry gray __(9)__ came to Pig's house. Clever Pig decided to __(10)__ that he was a piggy bank. He sat very still, which took all of his __(11)__. It worked! The wolf gave an angry __(12)__ and left. "I'm hungry," said the wolf, "but I'm not a bank robber!"

9. _____

10. _____

11. _____

12. _____

Name _____

Spelling and Writing

SPELLING WORDS			
water	little	enter	grandmother
other	under	candle	tumble

Writer's Words from the Story	
wolf	pretend
growl	strength

Video Time Pretend that you have made a video of the Lon Po Po story. Make an exciting poster for the video store window. Use sentences and pictures that will make people want to see your video. Use words from the lists above.

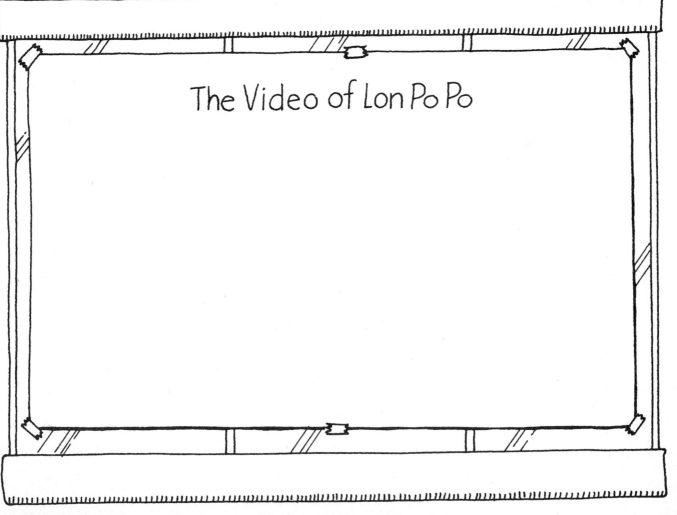

The Video of Lon Po Po

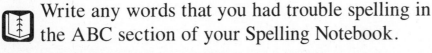

Write any words that you had trouble spelling in the ABC section of your Spelling Notebook.

SPELLING WORDS

1. cried
2. hurried
3. stories
4. tried
5. flies
6. puppies
7. carried
8. pennies

Your Own Words

What other words do you need to study for spelling? Add them to My Study List 15 on page 100.

Name _____

15 Changing Final y to i

Each Spelling Word is made up of a base word and the ending *-es* or *-ed*. When a base word ends with a consonant and *y*, change the *y* to *i* before adding *-es* or *-ed*.

$$story - y + ies = stories$$
$$cry - y + ied = cried$$

Water the Words Join the base word and ending on each flower to make a Spelling Word. Then write each Spelling Word on Abdul Gasazi's watering can.

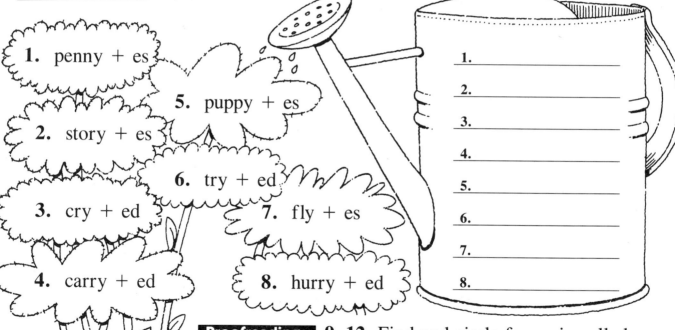

1. penny + es
2. story + es
3. cry + ed
4. carry + ed
5. puppy + es
6. try + ed
7. fly + es
8. hurry + ed

1. _____
2. _____
3. _____
4. _____
5. _____
6. _____
7. _____
8. _____

Proofreading 9–12. Find and circle four misspelled Spelling Words in these lines from a play. Then write each word correctly.

Who Did It? Act 1

Kim: Tim! Your pupies broke my jar of pennys.
Tim: They did not! I carreyed the dogs to my room and told them stories until bedtime.
Kim: Well, someone cryed, "Stop!"

---

9. _____
10. _____
11. _____
12. _____

Developing Meaning

Big Trouble Write a Spelling Word to complete the answer to each question.

1. What did you do when you lost your favorite toy?
   I ___ great big tears.
2. What did you do when your cat was hurt?
   I ___ her carefully in my arms.
3. What did you do when the cup broke?
   I ___ to glue it back together.
4. What did you do when you overslept?
   I ___ to school as fast as I could.

1. _____   3. _____

2. _____   4. _____

SPELLING WORDS

1. cried
2. hurried
3. stories
4. tried
5. flies
6. puppies
7. carried
8. pennies

Writer's Words from the Story

9. leash
10. collar
11. tracks
12. warning

Classifying Write the Spelling Word that belongs in each group.

5. ponies, kittens, ___   7. dimes, nickels, ___
6. tales, fables, ___   8. walks, swims, ___

5. _____

6. _____

7. _____

8. _____

Walk the Dog Write the Writer's Words to complete the paragraph.

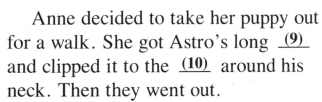

Anne decided to take her puppy out for a walk. She got Astro's long __(9)__ and clipped it to the __(10)__ around his neck. Then they went out.

After the walk, Astro ran into the house. He made muddy __(11)__ all over the rug. Oh dear! This morning Dad had given Anne a __(12)__ about what would happen if Astro did that again!

9. _____

10. _____

11. _____

12. _____

Spelling and Writing

SPELLING WORDS			
cried	stories	flies	carried
hurried	tried	puppies	pennies

Writer's Words from the Story	
leash	tracks
collar	warning

Problem Pets Fritz got Alan into trouble when he ran into Abdul Gasazi's garden. Pretend that you have these pets. Write sentences that tell how they got you into trouble. Use words from the lists above.

1. I love my pet dog, but _____

_____

_____

_____

2. I love my pet monkey, but _____

_____

_____

_____

Now choose a naughty pet yourself. Draw its picture in the space below the other pictures.

3. I love my pet _____, but _____

_____

_____

_____

Write any words that you had trouble spelling in the ABC section of your Spelling Notebook.

Name _____

Spelling Review

Write Spelling Words from the list on this page to answer each question.

 final |ē| hap**py**, bab**y**

1–4. Which four words have the final |ē| sound spelled *y*?

1. _____   3. _____

2. _____   4. _____

 final |ər| sounds   wat**er**
final |əl| sounds   can**dle**

5–7. Which three words end with the |ər| sounds?

5. _____   7. _____

6. _____

8–9. Which two words end with the |əl| sounds?

8. _____   9. _____

 penny − y + ies = penn**ies**
cry − y + ied = cr**ied**

10–12. In which three words does the final *y* change to *i* before *-es* or *-ed* is added?

10. _____   12. _____

11. _____

SPELLING WORDS

- hurried
- other
- only
- tried
- enter
- very
- tumble
- under
- funny
- little
- any
- stories

Beware! Enter at your own risk!

Name _____

Spelling Spree

Write Spelling Words from the list on this page to complete the activity.

Garden Game Follow Fritz into the garden. Write a word to complete each sentence on the game board. The pictures are clues. Go through the gate to win!

1. Get ____ to begin!

2. Wade across the ____.

12. Open the big ____ gate.

3. Feed the ____.

11. Pay two ____.

4. Oh no! She ____.

10. Look ____. You are close.

5. Light the ____.

9. Pick some flowers for your ____.

You are in the garden!

6. Pat the ____.

8. A duck ____ over. Duck!

7. It's raining! You should have ____ an umbrella.

1. _____
2. _____
3. _____
4. _____
5. _____
6. _____
7. _____
8. _____
9. _____
10. _____
11. _____
12. _____

STUDENT'S HANDBOOK

SPELLING NOTEBOOK

TAKE-HOME LISTS

Proofreading Checklist

Ask yourself each question. Check your paper for mistakes. Correct any mistakes you find. Put a check in the box when you find no more mistakes.

- ☐ **1.** Did I indent each paragraph?
- ☐ **2.** Does each sentence tell one complete thought?
- ☐ **3.** Did I end each sentence with the correct mark?
- ☐ **4.** Did I begin each sentence with a capital letter?
- ☐ **5.** Did I use capital letters correctly in other places?
- ☐ **6.** Did I use commas correctly?
- ☐ **7.** Did I spell all the words the right way?

Is there anything else you should look for? Make your own proofreading list.

- ☐ _____
- ☐ _____

Proofreading Hints

1. Read each line one at a time. Put a strip of colored paper or cardboard under the line you are reading.
2. Touch each word with your finger.
3. Say each word out loud to yourself.
4. Put a check mark on each word.
5. Spell each letter in a word out loud to make sure there are no missing letters.
6. Read your paper aloud to a friend.
7. Have a friend proofread your paper.
8. Read your paper from right to left.
9. Circle and look up any word you are not sure of.

Proofreading Marks

Mark	Explanation	Example
¶	Begin a new paragraph. Indent the paragraph.	¶Whales are huge animals that live in the sea. Blue whales are the largest and can grow to be one hundred feet long.
∧	Add letters, words, or sentences.	Gray whales may be black or ∧dark gray.
℘	Take out words, sentences, and punctuation marks. Correct spelling.	Some whales, can hold their there breath up to seventy-five minutes.
/	Change a capital letter to a small letter.	A baby whale stays close to its Mother for about a year.
≡	Change a small letter to a capital letter.	Humpback whales live off the coast of maine.

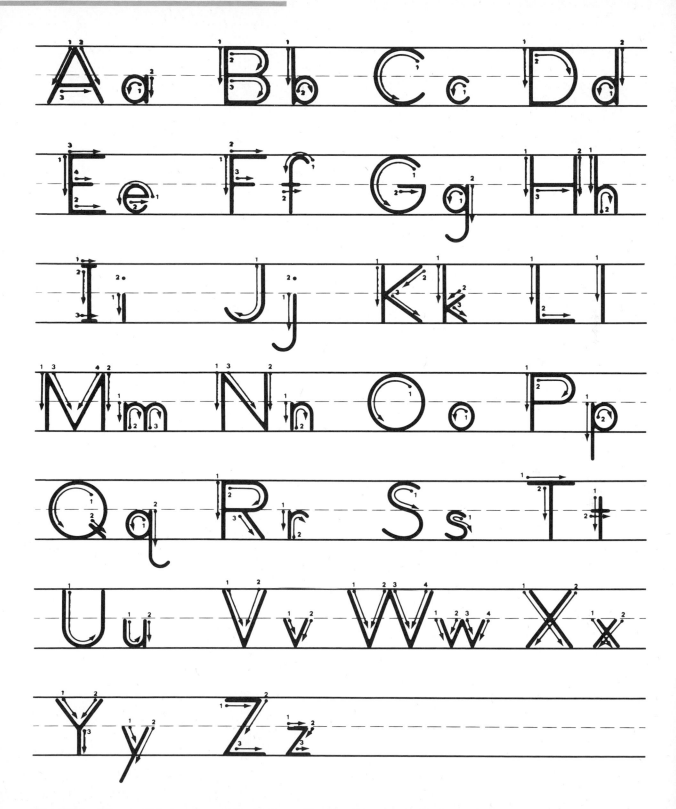

The Zaner-Bloser alphabet is reprinted from *Handwriting: Basic Skills and Application*. Copyright © 1989. Reprinted with permission of Zaner-Bloser, Inc., Columbus, OH.

The Zaner-Bloser alphabet is reprinted from *Handwriting: Basic Skills and Application*. Copyright © 1989. Reprinted with permission of Zaner-Bloser, Inc., Columbus, OH.

Handwriting style from HBJ HANDWRITING by Betty Kracht Johnson, copyright © 1987 by Harcourt Brace Jovanovich, Inc., reprinted by permission of the publisher.

Aa Bb Cc Dd

Ee Ff Gg Hh

Ii Jj Kk Ll

Mm Nn Oo Pp

Qq Rr Ss Tt

Uu Vv Ww Xx

Yy Zz

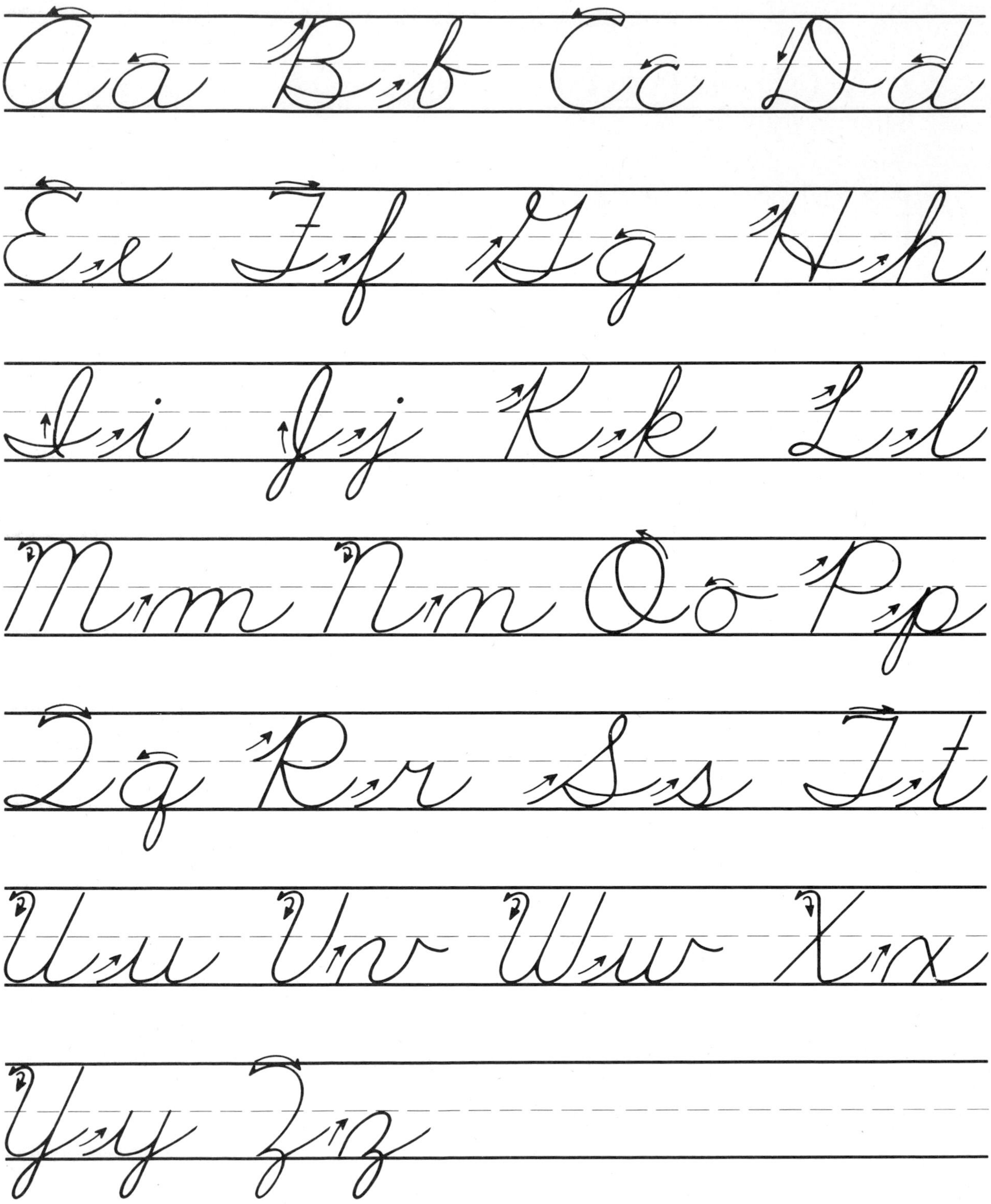

Handwriting style from HBJ HANDWRITING by Betty Kracht Johnson, copyright © 1987 by Harcourt Brace Jovanovich, Inc., reprinted by permission of the publisher.

The McDougal, Littell alphabet is used with permission from *McDougal, Littell Handwriting*. Copyright © 1990 by McDougal, Littell and Company, Evanston, Illinois.

Handwriting Models

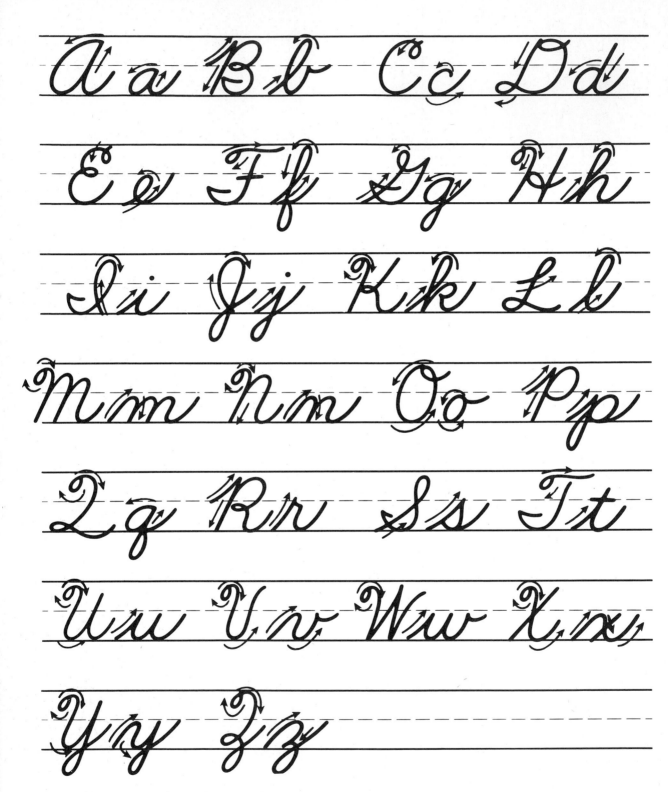

The McDougal, Littell alphabet is used with permission from *McDougal, Littell Handwriting*. Copyright © 1990 by McDougal, Littell and Company, Evanston, Illinois.

Handwriting Models

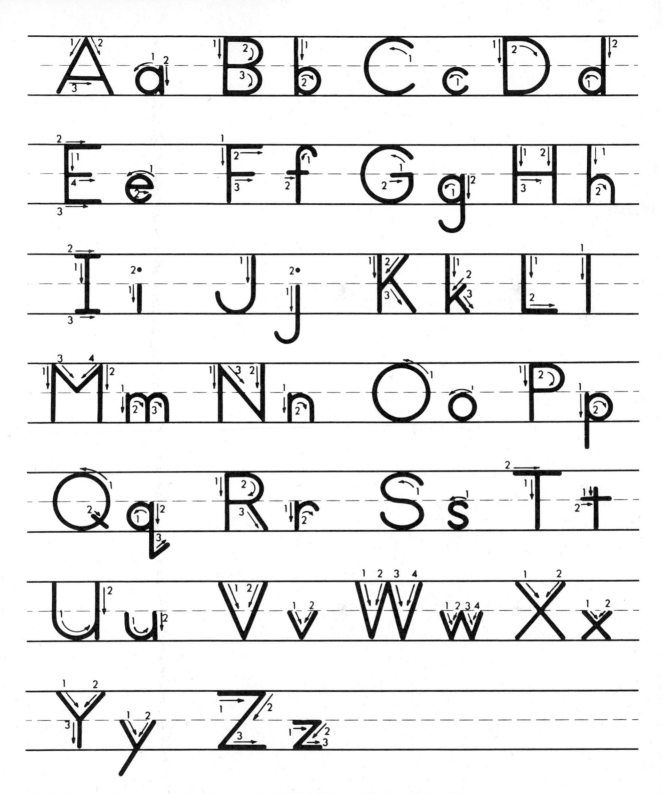

The Palmer alphabet is reprinted with permission of Macmillan/McGraw-Hill School Publishing Company from *Palmer Method Handwriting*, Centennial Edition. Copyright © 1987 by Macmillan Publishing Company.

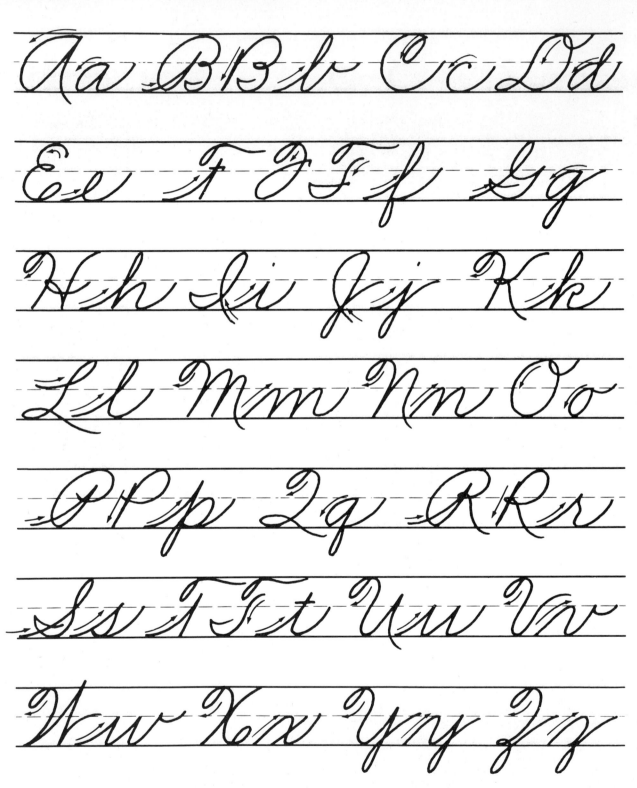

The Palmer alphabet is reprinted with permission of Macmillan/McGraw-Hill School Publishing Company from *Palmer Method Handwriting*, Centennial Edition. Copyright © 1987 by Macmillan Publishing Company.

Spelling Table.....................

This Spelling Table shows many of the letter combinations that spell the same sounds in different words. Use it to look up words you cannot spell.

Sounds	Spellings	Sample Words
|ă|	a, au	bat, have, laugh
|ā|	a, ai, ay, ea, eigh, ey	tale, later, rain, pay, great, eight, they
|âr|	air, are, ear, eir, ere	fair, care, bear, their, where
|ä|	a, al	father, calm
|är|	ar	art
|b|	b, bb	bus, rabbit
|ch|	ch, tch	chin, match
|d|	d, dd	dark, sudden
|ĕ|	a, ai, e, ea, ie	any, said, went, head, friend
|ē|	e, ea, ee, ey, y	these, we, beast, tree, honey, lady
|f|	f, ff, gh	funny, off, enough
|g|	g, gg	get, egg
|h|	h, wh	hat, who
|hw|	wh	when
|ĭ|	e, ee, i, ui, y	before, been, mix, give, build, gym
|ī|	i, ie, igh, uy, y	time, mind, pie, fight, buy, try
|îr|	ear, ere	near, here
|j|	dge, g, ge, j	judge, gym, age, jet
|k|	c, ch, ck, k	picnic, school, stick, keep
|kw|	qu	quick
|l|	l, ll	last, all
|m|	m, mm	mop, summer
|n|	kn, n, nn	knee, nine, penny
|ng|	n, ng	think, ring
|ŏ|	a, o	was, pond

Sounds	Spellings	Sample Words
|ō|	ew, o, oa, oe, ough, ow	sew, most, hope, float, toe, though, row
|ô|	a, a before l, aw, o, ough, augh	wall, talk, lawn, soft, brought, caught
|ôr|	oor, or, ore	door, storm, store
|oi|	oi, oy	join, toy
|ou|	ou, ow	loud, now
|o͝o|	oo, ou, u	good, could, put
|o͞o|	ew, o, oe, oo, ou, ough, u, ue	flew, do, shoe, spoon, you, through, flute, blue
|p|	p, pp	paint, happen
|r|	r, wr	rub, write
|s|	c, s, ss	city, same, grass
|sh|	s, sh	sure, sheep
|t|	ed, t, tt	fixed, tall, kitten
|th|	th	they
|th|	th	thin, teeth
|ŭ|	o, oe, u	front, come, does, sun
|yo͞o|	ew, u	few, use
|ûr|	ear, er, ir, or, ur	learn, herd, girl, word, turn
|v|	f, v	of, very
|w|	o, w	one, way
|y|	y	yes
|z|	s, z	please, zoo
|zh|	s	usual
|ə|	a, e, i, o, u	about, silent, pencil, lemon, circus

How to Use a Dictionary ....

Finding an Entry Word

Guide Words

The word you want to find in a dictionary is listed in ABC order. To find it quickly, turn to the part of the dictionary that has words with the same first letter. Use the guide words at the top of each page for help. Guide words name the first entry word and the last entry word on each page.

Base Words

To find a word ending in **-ed** or **-ing,** you usually must look up its base word. To find **filled** or **filling,** for example, look up the base word **fill.**

Reading an Entry

Read the dictionary entry below. Look carefully at each part of the entry.

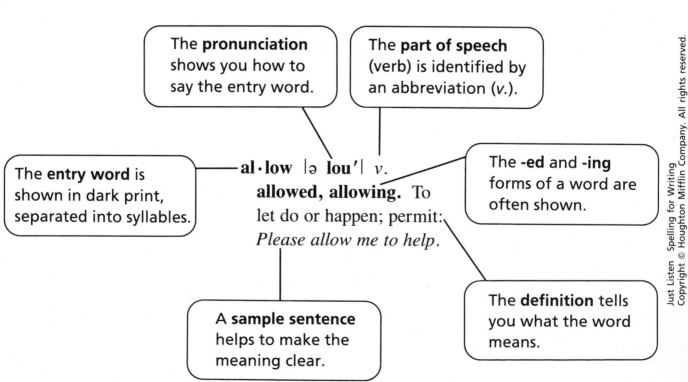

The **pronunciation** shows you how to say the entry word.

The **part of speech** (verb) is identified by an abbreviation (*v.*).

The **entry word** is shown in dark print, separated into syllables.

al·low |ə lou′| *v.* **allowed, allowing.** To let do or happen; permit: *Please allow me to help.*

The **-ed** and **-ing** forms of a word are often shown.

The **definition** tells you what the word means.

A **sample sentence** helps to make the meaning clear.

Spelling Dictionary ······················

This dictionary contains every **Spelling Word, Writer's Word,** and **Challenge Word** in your *Spelling for Writing* booklet. The definitions given here will help you complete the booklet activities. Use your classroom dictionary to explore additional words and meanings.

Pronunciation Key

ă	pat	ŏ	pot	û	fur
ā	pay	ō	go	*th*	the
â	care	ô	paw, for	th	thin
ä	father	oi	oil	hw	which
ĕ	pet	͞o͞o	book	zh	usual
ē	be	o͞o	boot	ə	ago, item
ĭ	pit	yo͞o	cute		pencil, atom
ī	ice	ou	out		circus
î	near	ŭ	cut	ər	butter

Abbreviation Key

n.	noun	*p.*	past
v.	verb	*p. part.*	past participle
adj.	adjective	*prep.*	preposition
adv.	adverb	*interj.*	interjection
pron.	pronoun	*sing.*	singular
conj.	conjunction	*pl.*	plural

A

a·gree |ə **grē′**| *v.* **agreed, agreeing.** To have or share the same opinion: *Ann and I agreed that our school was the best.*

al·low |ə **lou′**| *v.* **allowed, allowing.** To let do or happen; permit: *Please allow me to help.*

al·read·y |ôl **rĕd′** ē| *adv.* By this time: *I already ate my lunch.*

al·though |ôl **thō′**| *conj.* Even though.

an·cient |**ān′** shənt| *adj.* Having to do with times long past: *I love stories of people who lived in ancient times.*

an·swer |**ăn′** sər| *n., pl.* **answers.** Something said or written in return to a question, statement, or letter; reply.

an·y |**ĕn′** ē| *adj.* One or some: *Take any book you want.*

an·y·one |**ĕn′** ē wŭn′| *pron.* Any person; anybody: *I didn't know anyone at the dance.*

art·ist |**är′** tĭst| *n., pl.* **artists.** One who practices an art, such as painting or music: *The artist drew pictures of wild animals.*

a·while |ə **whīl′**| *adv.* For a short time: *Let's wait awhile.*

B

ba·by |**bā′** bē| *n., pl.* **babies.** A very young child; infant.

ball |bôl| *n., pl.* **balls.** A round object used in a game or sport.

bas·ket |**băs′** kĭt| *n., pl.* **baskets.** A container made of woven grasses or strips of wood.

beg |bĕg| *v.* **begged, begging.** To ask earnestly as a favor.

bought |bôt| *v.* Past tense and past participle of **buy:** *They bought a house.*

bow |bou| *n., pl.* **bows.** A bending of the body or head, as when showing respect or thanks: *Take a bow at the end of the play.*

boy |boi| *n., pl.* **boys.** A young male person.

bread |brĕd| *n., pl.* **breads.** A food made from flour that is mixed with water or milk. It is kneaded and baked.

break·fast |**brĕk′** fəst| *n., pl.* **breakfasts.** The first meal of the day.

brit·tle |**brĭt′** l| *adj.* Hard and easily broken: *The brittle branch snapped off the tree.*

buy |bī| *v.* **bought** |bôt|, **buying.** To get by paying the price for: *We bought a new car.*

Spelling Dictionary

C

cac·tus |kăk′ təs| *n., pl.* **cacti** |kăk′ tī| *or* **cactuses.** One of many kinds of plants that have thick, often spiny stems without leaves and that grow in hot, dry places.

can·dle |kăn′ dl| *n., pl.* **candles.** A solid stick of wax with a wick inside that is lit and burned to give light.

card·board |kärd′ bôrd′| *n.* A stiff, heavy paper used for making cards, boxes, and posters.

car·ry |kăr′ ē| *v.* **carried, carrying.** To take from one place to another: *I carried the books to the library.*

catch |kăch| *v.* **caught** |kôt|, **catching.** To get hold of or grasp something that is moving; sieze: *Betsy tossed a pen to me, and I caught it.*

caught |kôt| *v.* Past tense and past participle of **catch:** *He caught the falling vase.*

cel·e·brate |sĕl′ ə brāt′| *v.* **celebrated, celebrating.** To have a party or other such activity to honor a special occasion.

chop |chŏp| *v.* **chopped, chopping. 1.** To cut by striking with a heavy, sharp tool, such as an ax: *The lumberjacks were chopping down trees.* **2.** To cut up into small pieces.

clev·er |klĕv′ ər| *adj.* **cleverer, cleverest.** Having or showing a quick mind; smart.

close |klōz| *v.* **closed, closing.** To shut: *The rain began just as I closed the window.*

coat |kōt| *n., pl.* **coats.** A piece of clothing with sleeves, usually worn outdoors over other clothes.

cof·fee |kô′ fē| *n.* A drink prepared from the ground roasted seeds of a tropical tree.

coin |koin| *n., pl.* **coins.** A piece of metal used as money, such as a penny or a dime.

col·lar |kŏl′ ər| *n., pl.* **collars.** A leather or metal band for the neck of an animal.

cop·y |kŏp′ ē| *v.* **copied, copying.** To make something look exactly like something else: *She copied my hair style.*

count |kount| *v.* **counted, counting.** To find the total of; add up.

crowd |kroud| *n., pl.* **crowds.** A large number of people gathered together.

crumb |krŭm| *n., pl.* **crumbs.** A tiny piece of food, especially of bread or cake.

crust |krŭst| *n., pl.* **crusts.** The hard outer layer of bread: *The crust is golden brown when the bread is done.*

cry |krī| *v.* **cried, crying. 1.** To shed tears; weep. **2.** To call loudly; shout: *We cried a warning, but they did not hear us.*

cur·tain |kûr′ tn| *n., pl.* **curtains.** A piece of material hanging in a window or other opening.

cus·tom |kus′ təm| *n., pl.* **customs. 1.** Something that the members of a group usually do: *Celebrating the first day of spring is an ancient custom.* **2.** Something that a person does all the time; habit: *Our custom is to vacation at a ranch every summer.*

D

dain·ty |dān′ tē| *adj.* Lovely, in a fine, delicate way: *The baby's clothes are very dainty.*

dance |dăns| *v.* **danced, dancing.** To move the feet and hands, usually in time to music.

daugh·ter |dô′ tər| *n., pl.* **daughters.** A female offspring or child.

deaf |dĕf| *adj.* Unable to hear.

dec·o·rate |dĕk′ ə rāt′| *v.* **decorated, decorating.** To make something attractive or beautiful: *Let's decorate the cake.*

Spelling Dictionary

de·light |dĭ **līt′**| *n.* Great pleasure: *She smiled with delight.*

den·tist |**dĕn′** tĭst| *n., pl.* **dentists.** A person who takes care of teeth.

die |dī| *v.* **died, dying.** To stop living; become dead: *The flowers will die in the fall.*

din·ner |**dĭn′** ər| *n., pl.* **dinners.** The main meal of the day.

dis·ap·pear |dĭs ə **pîr′**| *v.* **disappeared, disappearing.** To pass out of sight; vanish.

dive |dīv| *v.* **dived** *or* **dove** |dōv|, **diving.** **1.** To plunge or leap into water with the head first. **2.** To plunge downward at a steep angle: *I saw the eagle diving through the sky.*

doc·tor |**dŏk′** tər| *n., pl.* **doctors.** A person whose job is to help sick people get well.

doubt |dout| *v.* **doubted, doubting.** To have no trust in: *Do you doubt my story?*

dough |dō| *n.* A soft, thick mixture made of flour and liquids that is used to make bread and baked goods.

draw·ing |**drô′** ĭng| *n.* The art of making a picture with lines: *Drawing animals is her favorite hobby.*

drop |drŏp| *v.* **dropped, dropping.** To fall or let fall: *The apples dropped to the ground when I shook the tree.*

du·ty |**doo′** tē| *or* |**dyoo′** tē| *n., pl.* **duties.** Something that a person must do as part of his or her job: *The class president has certain duties to carry out.*

E

emp·ty |**ĕmp′** tē| *adj.* **emptier, emptiest.** Having nothing inside.

en·joy |ĕn **joi′**| *v.* **enjoyed, enjoying.** To get pleasure from: *I enjoy sports.*

en·ter |**ĕn′** tər| *v.* **entered, entering.** To come or go into: *Please enter by the front door.*

es·cape |ĭ **skāp′**| *v.* **escaped, escaping.** To get free: *How did the dog escape from the yard?*

eve·ry·bod·y |**ĕv′** rē bŏd′ ē| *pron.* Every person; everyone.

Pronunciation Key

ă	pat	ŏ	pot	û	fur
ā	pay	ō	go	*th*	the
â	care	ô	paw, for	th	thin
ä	father	oi	oil	hw	which
ĕ	pet	o͞o	book	zh	usual
ē	be	o͞o	boot	ə	ago, item
ĭ	pit	yo͞o	cute		pencil, atom
ī	ice	ou	out		circus
î	near	ŭ	cut	ər	butter

ex·pect |ĭk **spĕkt′**| *v.* **expected, expecting.** To look for as likely to happen: *I expect you to go with me.*

ex·plain |ĭk **splān′**| *v.* **explained, explaining.** To make clear: *Please explain that math problem to me.*

F

face |fās| *n., pl.* **faces.** The front part of the head from the forehead to the chin.

fall |fôl| *v.* **fell** |fĕl|, **falling.** To drop or come down: *The leaf fell from the tree.*

false |fôls| *adj.* **falser, falsest.** Not true, real, honest, or correct.

fa·vor·ite |**fā′** vər ĭt′| *adj.* Liked above all others.

fell |fĕl| *v.* Past tense and past participle of **fall:** *I fell off my bicycle.*

fill |fĭl| *v.* **filled, filling.** To make full: *Please fill my glass with milk.*

float |flōt| *v.* **floated, floating.** To be held up in or at the top of water or air: *I can float on my back in the pool.*

fly |flī| *v.* **flew** |floo|, **flying.** To move through the air with wings: *A plane flies over our house each day.*

fol·low·ing |**fŏl′** ō ĭng| *adj.* Coming after; next: *He left on Friday, and I left the following day.*

for·ev·er |fər **ĕv′** ər| *adv.* For all time; always.

fright·en |**frīt′** n| *v.* **frightened, frightening.** To make or become afraid.

fun·ny |**fŭn′** ē| *adj.* **funnier, funniest.** Causing amusement or laughter; not serious.

Spelling Dictionary

G

game |gām| *n., pl.* **games.** A sport or other form of play carried on according to a special set of rules: *Do you want to join our softball game?*

gift |gĭft| *n., pl.* **gifts.** Something given; present.

grand·fa·ther |grănd' fä' thər| *n., pl.* **grandfathers.** The father of one's father or mother.

grand·moth·er |grănd' mŭ' thər| *n., pl.* **grandmothers.** The mother of one's father or mother.

green |grēn| *n.* The color of most plant leaves and growing grass. —*adj.* **greener, greenest.** Of the color green: *That is a pretty green sweater.*

growl |groul| *v.* **growled, growling.** A low, deep, angry sound, as the one made by a dog.

H

Hal·low·een |hăl' ə wēn'| *or* |hŏl' ə wēn'| *n.* October 31, a holiday that children celebrate by wearing masks and costumes and by asking for treats.

hap·pen |hăp' ən| *v.* **happened, happening.** To take place by accident or chance: *Did you happen to find my missing sock?*

hap·py |hăp' ē| *adj.* **happier, happiest.** Showing or feeling joy; glad.

heav·y |hĕv' ē| *adj.* **heavier, heaviest.** Weighing a lot.

huge |hyōōj| *adj.* **huger, hugest.** Very big; enormous.

hun·gry |hŭng' grē| *adj.* **hungrier, hungriest.** Wanting food.

hur·ry |hûr' ē| *v.* **hurried, hurrying.** To act or move quickly; rush: *I hurried home.*

I

im·pos·si·ble |ĭm pŏs' ə bəl| *adj.* Not likely to happen or be done.

in·side |ĭn' sīd| *or* |ĭn sīd'| *adv.* Into; within: *I'm staying inside today.*

in·to |ĭn' tōō| *prep.* Toward the inside.

in·vite |ĭn vīt'| *v.* **invited, inviting.** To ask someone to come somewhere or do something: *Did you invite her to lunch?*

J

jam |jăm| *n., pl.* **jams.** A sweet food made by boiling fruit and sugar together until the mixture is thick: *I made a sandwich with peanut butter and jam.*

jaw |jô| *n., pl.* **jaws.** The parts of the face that hold the teeth and form the shape of the mouth. The upper and lower jaws are made of bone.

L

lay |lā| *v.* Past tense of **lie**: *The coat lay on the chair for three days.*

leash |lēsh| *n., pl.* **leashes.** A cord, chain, or strap attached to a collar or harness. It is used to hold or lead an animal.

leave |lēv| *v.* **left** |lĕft|, **leaving. 1.** To go away from: *I must leave the house now.* **2.** To let stay behind: *Please don't leave the dog alone.*

leg·end |lĕj' ənd| *n., pl.* **legends.** A story handed down from earlier times. A legend is often believed by many people, but its truth is uncertain.

lie |lī| *v.* **lay** |lā|, **lying.** To rest on a flat or horizontal surface: *The books lay on the floor.*

lit·tle |lĭt' l| *adj.* **littler, littlest.** Small.

lunch |lŭnch| *n., pl.* **lunches.** A meal eaten around noon.

M

mag·ic |măj' ĭk| *n.* The art of doing tricks that seem impossible.

mail |māl| *n.* **1.** Items, such as letters and post cards, that are sent from one place to another through a government's postal system: *Do you need stamps for your mail?* **2.** A delivery of mail: *What did we get in the mail today?* —*v.* **mailed, mailing.** To send through the postal system.

mar·vel |mär' vəl| *v.* **marveled, marveling.** To be filled with surprise or wonder.

ma·te·ri·al |mə tîr' ē əl| *n., pl.* **materials.** Cloth or fabric: *Cotton is one type of material.*

may·be |mā' bē| *adv.* Possibly; perhaps: *Maybe we can go skating today.*

mer·cy |mûr' sē| *n., pl.* **mercies.** Great kindness: *The boy had mercy on the mouse and let it go.*

mis·take |mĭ stāk'| *n., pl.* **mistakes.** Something that is not done correctly.

move |mo͞ov| *v.* **moved, moving.** To change or cause to change position: *The train began moving.*

N

need |nēd| *n., pl.* **needs.** A lack of something that is necessary or wanted: *Their crops are in need of water.* —*v.* **needed, needing.** **1.** To have to: *You need to hurry or you will be late.* **2.** To have need of: *I need a bigger box.*

next |nĕkst| *adj.* Coming right after, as in space or time: *I was next in line.*

Pronunciation Key

ă	pat	ŏ	pot	û	fur
ā	pay	ō	go	*th*	the
â	care	ô	paw, for	th	thin
ä	father	oi	oil	hw	which
ĕ	pet	o͞o	book	zh	usual
ē	be	o͞o	boot	ə	ago, item
ĭ	pit	yo͞o	cute		pencil, atom
ī	ice	ou	out		circus
î	near	ŭ	cut	ər	butter

nice |nīs| *adj.* **nicer, nicest.** Pleasant; agreeable; not nasty: *She is a very nice person.*

night |nīt| *n., pl.* **nights.** The time between sunset and sunrise, especially the hours of darkness.

noise |noiz| *n., pl.* **noises.** **1.** A loud or unpleasant sound. **2.** Any kind of sound.

noth·ing |nŭth' ĭng| *pron.* Not anything: *There is nothing to say.*

no·tice |nō' tĭs| *v.* **noticed, noticing.** To pay attention to: *No one noticed the little mouse.*

num·ber |nŭm' bər| *n., pl.* **numbers.** **1.** A symbol or word used in counting: *Ten is a number.* **2.** A numeral given to something to identify it: *This is game number ten.*

O

of·fice |ô' fĭs| *n., pl.* **offices.** A place in which work or business is carried on: *My dentist's office has three rooms.*

on·ly |ōn' lē| *adv.* As recently as: *I saw them only yesterday.*

oth·er |ŭth' ər| *pron.* **1.** Being the remaining one or ones: *I cannot find my other glove.* **2.** Different: *Call me some other time.*

out·side |out sīd'| *adv.* Away from the inside; outdoors.

own |ōn| *adj.* Of or belonging to oneself: *Do you have your own room?* —*v.* **owned, owning.** To have or possess: *I own a blue car.*

Spelling Dictionary

P

pen·ny |pĕn′ ē| *n., pl.* **pennies.** A coin used in the United States and Canada; cent: *I have pennies, dimes, and nickels in my piggy bank.*

per·form |pər fôrm′| *v.* **performed, performing.** To present, especially before an audience: *The magician will perform many tricks tonight.*

plan |plăn| *v.* **planned, planning.** To have in mind; intend: *We planned to leave at two o'clock.*

plant |plănt| *v.* **planted, planting.** To put in the ground or in soil to grow. *Next year you can plant more tulips around the tree.*

please |plēz| *v.* To be willing to do something: *Pass the jam, please.*

plum |plŭm| *n., pl.* **plums.** A small fruit with a pit and red, purple, or yellow skin. Plums grow on small trees.

pol·ish |pŏl′ ĭsh| *v.* **polished, polishing.** To make smooth and shiny, especially by rubbing. *To make the shoes look new again, polish them.*

prac·tice |prăk′ tĭs| *n., pl.* **practices.** Action done over and over in order to develop or improve a skill: *I have an hour of piano practice every day.*

pre·pare |prĭ pâr′| *v.* **prepared, preparing.** To put together the ingredients of: *We prepared the bread dough.*

pre·tend |prĭ tĕnd′| *v.* **pretended, pretending.** To make believe.

pup·py |pŭp′ ē| *n., pl.* **puppies.** A young dog.

put |po͝ot| *v.* **put, putting.** To place in a certain spot: *I am putting the bowl on the table.*

Q

quilt |kwĭlt| *n., pl.* **quilts.** A bed covering made by sewing together two layers of cloth with a warm layer of cotton or feathers between them.

R

rab·bit |răb′ ĭt| *n., pl.* **rabbits.** A burrowing animal with long ears, soft fur, and a short furry tail.

raw |rô| *adj.* **rawer, rawest.** Not cooked.

read·y |rĕd′ ē| *adv.* **readier, readiest.** Prepared for action or use.

re·mem·ber |rĭ mĕm′ bər| *v.* **remembered, remembering.** To keep carefully in one's memory.

re·ply |rĭ plī′| *v.* **replied, replying.** To say or give an answer: *I replied that I would go.*

S

sand·wich |sănd′ wĭch| *n., pl.* **sandwiches.** Two or more slices of bread with a filling of food between them.

save |sāv| *v.* **saved, saving. 1.** To rescue from danger or loss. **2.** To keep from wasting or spending: *Riding my bike to school saved me a lot of time.*

scene |sēn| *n., pl.* **scenes.** A place as seen by a viewer; view: *The scene before us was beautiful.*

se·cret |sē′ krĭt| *n., pl.* **secrets.** Something that is kept hidden or is known only to a few.

sew |sō| *v.* **sewed, sewing.** To put together with stitches made by a needle and thread.

shal·low |shăl′ ō| *adj.* **shallower, shallowest.** Not deep.

Spelling Dictionary

side |sīd| *n., pl.* **sides. 1.** One of the surfaces of an object that connects the top and bottom: *An ant crawled up the side of the house.* **2.** One of two or more opposing teams: *Our side won the basketball game.*

sign |sīn| *n., pl.* **signs.** An action or hand movement that gives information: *We are learning sign language in school.*

snow |snō| *n., pl.* **snows.** Soft white pieces of ice that come from clouds and fall to earth as frozen flakes.

some·thing |sŭm′ thĭng| *pron.* A thing that is not named: *I saw something new today.*

some·times |sŭm′ tīmz′| *adv.* Now and then; at times.

sound |sound| *n., pl.* **sounds.** Something that is heard.

speak |spēk| *v.* **spoke** |spōk|, **spoken, speaking.** To say words; talk: *She spoke in a loud voice.*

spoke |spōk| *v.* Past tense of **speak:** *I spoke to my aunt last night.*

square |skwâr| *n., pl.* **squares.** Anything in a shape having four equal sides.

sto·ry |stôr′ ē| *n., pl.* **stories.** A tale made up to entertain people: *He writes funny stories.*

straw |strô| *n., pl.* **straws. 1.** Stalks of grain, such as wheat or oats, whose seeds have been removed: *The bird used straw to make its nest.* **2.** A thin tube made of paper or plastic through which a person can drink a liquid.

strength |strĕngkth| *n.* The quality of being strong; power.

stunt |stŭnt| *n., pl.* **stunts.** A kind of trick that shows unusual skill.

sum·mer |sŭm′ ər| *n., pl.* **summers.** The hottest season of the year, between spring and autumn.

Sun·day |sŭn′ dē| *or* |sŭn′ dā| *n., pl.* **Sundays.** The first day of the week.

sup·ply |sə plī′| *n., pl.* **supplies.** Necessary materials kept and used or given out when needed: *We keep our gardening supplies in the basement.*

sur·prise |sər prīz′| *v.* **surprised, surprising.** To cause someone to wonder: *I was surprised at how young he looked.*

Pronunciation Key

ă	pat	ŏ	pot	û	fur
ā	pay	ō	go	*th*	the
â	care	ô	paw, for	th	thin
ä	father	oi	oil	hw	which
ĕ	pet	o͝o	book	zh	usual
ē	be	o͞o	boot	ə	ago, item
ĭ	pit	yo͞o	cute		pencil, atom
ī	ice	ou	out		circus
î	near	ŭ	cut	ər	butter

T

take |tāk| *v.* **took** |to͝ok|, **taken** |tā′ kən|, **taking. 1.** To get possession or use of: *Stop taking my books without asking.* **2.** To carry along with one: *I am taking my lunch with me today.*

taught |tôt| Past tense and past participle of **teach:** *Who taught you how to play the flute?*

teach |tēch| *v.* **taught** |tôt|, **teaching. 1.** To give lessons in. **2.** To show by example or experience: *I taught myself how to swim.*

tel·e·phone |tĕl′ ə fōn′| *n., pl.* **telephones.** An instrument that carries and receives sound, especially speech. The sound is carried over wires by electricity. *The telephone in our living room is my father's office line.*

ten·der |tĕn′ dər| *adj.* **tenderer, tenderest.** Not tough: *We cooked the carrots until they were tender.*

think |thĭngk| *v.* **thought** |thôt|, **thinking.** To use one's mind to form ideas and make decisions: *He thought a moment before deciding what to do.*

thought |thôt| *v.* Past tense and past participle of **think:** *I thought about going to the movies.*

thou·sand |thou′ zənd| *n., pl.* **thousands.** The number, written 1,000, that is equal to the product of 10 × 100. —*adj.* Being ten times one hundred.

Spelling Dictionary

tie |tī| *v.* **tied, tying. 1.** To fasten with a cord or rope. **2.** To fasten by drawing together and knotting strings or laces.

tight |tīt| *adj.* **tighter, tightest. 1.** Held or closed firmly in place; not loose: *He tied his shoelaces in a tight knot.* **2.** Fitting close or too close to the skin; snug: *These gloves are too tight.*

toy |toi| *n., pl.* **toys.** Something that children play with.

track |trăk| *n., pl.* **tracks.** A mark, such as a footprint, that is left behind by something that has moved by: *We saw rabbit tracks in the snow.*

train |trān| *n., pl.* **trains.** A string of connected railroad cars pulled by a locomotive or driven by electricity.

tray |trā| *n., pl.* **trays.** A flat, shallow container with a raised edge that is used for carrying or holding things: *I carried the glasses on a tray.*

trou·ble |trŭb' əl| *n., pl.* **troubles.** A difficult or dangerous situation.

try |trī| *v.* **tried, trying.** To make an effort; attempt: *We tried to be on time.*

tube |tōōb| *or* |tyōōb| *n., pl.* **tubes.** A soft container for such things as toothpaste and glue: *I squeezed the toothpaste from the tube.*

tum·ble |tŭm' bəl| *v.* **tumbled, tumbling.** To fall suddenly or roll end over end.

twen·ty |twĕn' tē| *n., pl.* **twenties.** The number, written 20, that is equal to the product of 2 × 10. —*adj.* Being one more than nineteen.

U

un·der |ŭn' dər| *prep.* Beneath and covered by; not over.

un·der·stand |ŭn' dər **stănd'**| *v.* **understood** |ŭn' dər **stood'**|, **understanding.** To get the meaning of: *Do you understand Spanish?*

V

van·ish |văn' ĭsh| *v.* **vanished, vanishing.** To disappear: *The magician's rabbit seemed to vanish into the air.*

ver·y |vĕr' ē| *adv.* To a high degree; extremely: *She was very happy about winning the game.*

vis·it |vĭz' ĭt| *n., pl.* **visits.** A stay as a guest: *My aunt came for a long visit.*

W

walk |wôk| *v.* **walked, walking.** To move on foot at an easy, steady pace.

warn·ing |wôr' nĭng| *n., pl.* **warnings.** Something that advises or cautions: *A red light is a warning to stop.*

wa·ter |wô' tər| *n.* The liquid that falls from the sky as rain and forms rivers, oceans, and lakes.

Wednes·day |wĕnz' dē| *or* |wĕnz' dā| *n., pl.* **Wednesdays.** The fourth day of the week.

whole |hōl| *adj.* **1.** Having no part missing; complete: *The whole class laughed.* **2.** Not divided; in one piece. —*n.* Something complete: *Two halves make a whole.*

wolf |woolf| *n., pl.* **wolves** |woolvz|. A wild animal that is related to the dog. Wolves often attack livestock but rarely bother people.

wor·ry |wûr' ē| *v.* **worried, worrying.** To feel or cause to feel uneasy: *I worry about my dog when he isn't hungry.*

SPELLING NOTEBOOK

Name

A

Words Often Misspelled

above
again
already
answer
any
are

B

Words Often Misspelled

bear
been
believe
beyond
blue
break
breath
brother
buy

C

Words Often Misspelled

ceiling
chief
children
choice
comb
come
cough
could
country

A B C D E F G H I J K L M N O P Q R S T U V

SPELLING NOTEBOOK

A B C D E F G H I J K L M N O P Q R S T U V W X

D

Words Often Misspelled

daily
dead
death
does
dollar
done
door
double
dying

E

Words Often Misspelled

early
electric
enough
eye

F

Words Often Misspelled

falling
feet
fought
friend
from
front

G

Words Often Misspelled

ghost
give
glove
gone
great
guess

H

Words Often Misspelled

half
have
head
heard
heart
heavy
helpful

I

Word Often Misspelled

island

J

Words Often Misspelled

judge
July
June

K

Word Often Misspelled

key

L

Words Often Misspelled

large
laugh
let's
libraries
listen
live
lose
love
lying

Just Listen Spelling for Writing

M

Words Often Misspelled

many
message
money
move

N

Words Often Misspelled

neighbor
noise
no one
none
nothing

O

Words Often Misspelled

o'clock
of
often
ought

A B C D E F G H I J K L M N O P Q R S T U V

P

Words Often Misspelled

pear
people
picnic
pink
pretty

Q

Words Often Misspelled

quiet
quit
quite

R

Words Often Misspelled

rebuild
roar
rolling
rough
rule

Just Listen Spelling for Writing
Copyright © Houghton Mifflin Company. All rights reserved.

S

Words Often Misspelled

said
school
sew
some
son
spread
straight
sure

T

Words Often Misspelled

tear
teeth
they
think
though
thought
toe
touch
trouble

U

Words Often Misspelled

until
unusual

V

Words Often Misspelled

voice

W

Words Often Misspelled

warm
was
watch
weigh
where
woman
wonderful
won't
word

XYZ

Words Often Misspelled

you
young
your

Just Listen Spelling for Writing
Copyright © Houghton Mifflin Company. All rights reserved.

Words from Social Studies

agriculture	forest	liberty	predator
climate	freight	mineral	recycling
coast	goods	monument	river
conservation	harbor	natural resource	shore
decompose	industry	pioneer	tepee
desert	inland	pollution	trade
environment	irrigation	population	transportation
fertilizer	island	prairie	wilderness

Words from Science

carbon dioxide	diet	habitat	saliva
circuit	digestion	hive	snowflake
cloud	erosion	lava	starch
constellation	fog	machine	stomach
crust	food chain	mold	telescope
cycle	fuel	muscle	vitamin
dam	gear	protein	volcano
dew	glacier	queen bee	water vapor

Words from Math

angle	digit	kilogram	product
area	factor	meter	quotient
average	Fahrenheit	minute	rectangle
Celsius	foot	numerator	remainder
cylinder	fraction	ounce	Roman numeral
decimal	gallon	perimeter	sphere
denominator	gram	pictograph	volume
diameter	graph	polygon	yard

Words from Language Arts

abbreviation	encyclopedia	noun	rhythm
adjective	exclamation	opinion	setting
alphabetical order	glossary	predicate	subject
antonym	homophone	pronoun	synonym
audience	index	proofread	thesaurus
command	instructions	publish	title
contrast	library	revise	verb
definition	nonfiction	rhyme	writer

Words from _____

Words from _____

Take-Home Word List 3

The Patchwork Quilt

Spelling Long a and Long e
$\vert\bar{a}\vert \rightarrow$ tr**ai**n, l**ay**
$\vert\bar{e}\vert \rightarrow$ pl**ea**se, n**ee**d

Spelling Words
1. need
2. please
3. green
4. lay
5. leave
6. train
7. tray
8. mail

Challenge Words
1. explain
2. agreed
3. Halloween
4. Wednesday

93

Take-Home Word List 2

Becky

Vowel-Consonant-e
$\vert\bar{a}\vert \rightarrow$ g**ame**
$\vert\bar{i}\vert \rightarrow$ n**ice**
$\vert\bar{o}\vert \rightarrow$ wh**ole**
$\vert\overline{oo}\vert$ or $\vert y\overline{oo}\vert \rightarrow$ t**ube**

Spelling Words
1. game
2. nice
3. face
4. whole
5. tube
6. side
7. spoke
8. huge

Challenge Words
1. awhile
2. surprise
3. mistake
4. telephone

93

Take-Home Word List 1

Jam

Short Vowels
$\vert\breve{a}\vert \rightarrow$ j**a**m
$\vert\breve{e}\vert \rightarrow$ n**e**xt
$\vert\breve{i}\vert \rightarrow$ f**i**ll
$\vert\breve{o}\vert \rightarrow$ dr**o**p
$\vert\breve{u}\vert \rightarrow$ pl**u**m

Spelling Words
1. fill
2. next
3. jam
4. fell
5. plum
6. plant
7. lunch
8. drop

Challenge Words
1. twenty
2. crumb
3. empty
4. sandwich

93

Name _____

📋 My Study List 1

Spelling Words

_____
_____
_____
_____
_____
_____
_____

Challenge Words

_____
_____
_____

My Own Words

_____
_____
_____

Name _____

📋 My Study List 2

Spelling Words

_____
_____
_____
_____
_____
_____
_____

Challenge Words

_____
_____
_____

My Own Words

_____
_____
_____

Name _____

📋 My Study List 3

Spelling Words

_____
_____
_____
_____
_____
_____
_____

Challenge Words

_____
_____
_____

My Own Words

_____
_____
_____

Take-Home Word List 7

Six Magic Tricks You Can Do

The Vowel Sound in ball

|ô| → str**aw**, b**a**ll
b**ough**t, c**augh**t

Spelling Words

1. walk
2. straw
3. raw
4. caught
5. ball
6. bought
7. taught
8. thought

Challenge Words

1. already
2. daughter
3. although
4. false

Take-Home Word List 6

The Floating Princess

The Vowel Sounds in count and boy

|ou| → cr**ow**d, c**ou**nt
|oi| → c**oi**n, b**oy**

Spelling Words

1. count
2. bow
3. boy
4. coin
5. toy
6. sound
7. crowd
8. noise

Challenge Words

1. enjoy
2. doubt
3. allow
4. thousand

Take-Home Word List 5

The Great Houdini

Spelling Long i and Long o

|ī| → t**igh**t, t**ie**
|ō| → c**oa**t, **ow**n

Spelling Words

1. tie
2. tight
3. coat
4. night
5. own
6. snow
7. die
8. float

Challenge Words

1. following
2. frighten
3. delight
4. shallow

Name _____

📃 My Study List 5

Spelling Words

_____
_____
_____
_____
_____
_____
_____

Challenge Words

_____
_____
_____

My Own Words

_____
_____
_____

Name _____

📃 My Study List 6

Spelling Words

_____
_____
_____
_____
_____
_____
_____

Challenge Words

_____
_____
_____

My Own Words

_____
_____
_____

Name _____

📃 My Study List 7

Spelling Words

_____
_____
_____
_____
_____
_____
_____

Challenge Words

_____
_____
_____

My Own Words

_____
_____
_____

Name _____

Take-Home Word List 11

And It Is Still That Way

Words Ending with -ed or -ing
drop + p + ed = dro**pped**
take − e + ing = tak**ing**

Spelling Words
1. taking
2. dropped
3. planned
4. diving
5. closed
6. begged
7. saved
8. chopping

Challenge Words
1. danced
2. moving
3. noticed
4. putting

97

Name _____

Take-Home Word List 10

The Farolitos of Christmas

Compound Words
may + **be** = maybe
in + **side** = inside

Spelling Words
1. grandfather
2. maybe
3. inside
4. outside
5. into
6. something
7. anyone
8. sometimes

Challenge Words
1. nothing
2. everybody
3. cardboard
4. breakfast

97

Name _____

Take-Home Word List 9

Family Pictures

The VCCV Pattern
VC | CV
i n | v i t e

Spelling Words
1. summer
2. Sunday
3. invite
4. dinner
5. happen
6. number
7. basket
8. rabbit

Challenge Words
1. custom
2. cactus
3. doctor
4. coffee

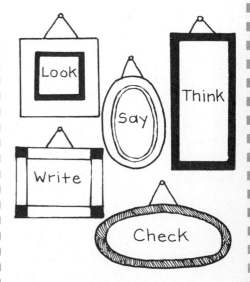

97

Name _____

📄 My Study List 9

Spelling Words

_____
_____
_____
_____
_____
_____

Challenge Words

_____
_____
_____

My Own Words

_____
_____
_____

98

Name _____

📄 My Study List 10

Spelling Words

_____
_____
_____
_____
_____
_____

Challenge Words

_____
_____
_____

My Own Words

_____
_____
_____

98

Name _____

📄 My Study List 11

Spelling Words

_____
_____
_____
_____
_____
_____

Challenge Words

_____
_____
_____

My Own Words

_____
_____
_____

98

Name _____

Take-Home Word List **15**

The Garden of Abdul Gasazi

Changing Final y to i
cry − y + ied = cr**ied**
fly − y + ies = fl**ies**

Spelling Words
1. cried
2. hurried
3. stories
4. tried
5. flies
6. puppies
7. carried
8. pennies

Challenge Words
1. copied
2. supplies
3. duties
4. replied

Name _____

Take-Home Word List **14**

Lon Po Po

Words That End with er or le
|ər| → wat**er**
|əl| → litt**le**

Spelling Words
1. water
2. other
3. little
4. under
5. enter
6. candle
7. grandmother
8. tumble

Challenge Words
1. answer
2. brittle
3. tender
4. trouble

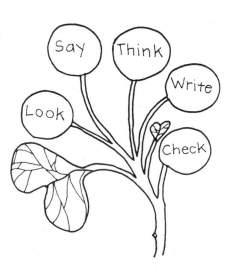

Name _____

Take-Home Word List **13**

Doctor De Soto

The Final Sound in happy
final |ē| → happ**y**, onl**y**

Spelling Words
1. happy
2. only
3. very
4. ready
5. any
6. heavy
7. baby
8. funny

Challenge Words
1. worry
2. dainty
3. mercy
4. hungry

Name _____

📃 My Study List 13

Spelling Words

_____
_____
_____
_____
_____
_____

Challenge Words

_____
_____
_____

My Own Words

_____
_____
_____

100

Name _____

📃 My Study List 14

Spelling Words

_____
_____
_____
_____
_____
_____

Challenge Words

_____
_____
_____

My Own Words

_____
_____
_____

100

Name _____

📃 My Study List 15

Spelling Words

_____
_____
_____
_____
_____
_____

Challenge Words

_____
_____
_____

My Own Words

_____
_____
_____

100